Praise for Mark Spitzer's *Beautifully Grotesque F*

"A certified angling addict, [Mark Spitzer] travels t
kinds of experiences that you're unlikely to find
of *Field & Stream*. . . . [His] shtick is to love the
the homely stalwarts that make up in resilience w
ventional beauty. . . . It's about embracing the natu
it looks like, wherever it swims."—Ben Goldfarb,

"This is a book that beautifully navigates the space
ment and information. Moments will stick with rea
them look at the fish and fisheries with new eyes."
Big Sky Journal

"Spitzer, like many of us, is looking for utility and fin
ness of underappreciated fish. The beautifully grotes
possibilities for us in our ever-changing world."—
Pacific Northwest Quarterly

"Reading this book is a little like sipping on an old, rich whi
interesting, and exactly what you need after a long da
—Joshua Peterson, *Casper Star Tribune*

"A powerful, beautiful, and ultimately kind book. We're l
—Max Wilson, *Lesser Places*

"[Spitzer's] a hard-core fisherman."—Daryl Bauer, Nebr
Parks Commission Fisheries Outreach Program manag

"Here is a book that captures that rhythm. Every page. The
will smile knowingly and follow Spitzer as he encounte
from endangered razorback suckers to burbot on ice. And
you'll realize you're enjoying a lot of science and conserva
—Matt Miller, *Cool Green Science*

"A w
the
Co

"Ma
an
co
ati

—
F

"M
la
w
v
r

IN SEARCH OF MONSTER FISH

IN
SEARCH *of*
MONSTER
FISH

Angling for a More Sustainable Planet

Mark Spitzer

UNIVERSITY OF NEBRASKA PRESS   *Lincoln*

Chapter 6 was originally published as "Monster Carp in
Manmade Reservoirs: In Pursuit of French Fish without
Borders" in *Spank the Carp*, no. 32 (September 2017).

Library of Congress Cataloging-in-Publication Data
Names: Spitzer, Mark, 1965– author.
Title: In search of monster fish: angling for a
more sustainable planet / Mark Spitzer.
Description: Lincoln: University of Nebraska Press,
[2019] | Includes bibliographical references.
Identifiers: LCCN 2018026901
ISBN 9781496211880 (cloth: alk. paper)
ISBN 9781496214294 (epub)
ISBN 9781496214300 (mobi)
ISBN 9781496214317 (pdf)
Subjects: LCSH: Fishing—Anecdotes. | Fishes—Size.
Classification: LCC SH441 .S748
2019 | DDC 639.2—dc23
LC record available at https://lccn.loc.gov/2018026901

Set in Janson by E. Cuddy.
Designed by N. Putens.

Fighting for the protection of our oceans is very much about fighting for our own survival. Paul [Watson] always says, "If the oceans die, we die." And for me, fighting to protect the ocean and its inhabitants is very much a matter of self-defense.
—Captain Peter Hammarstedt, *Whale Wars*, season 7, episode 1

In response to stress, biological survival requires genetic change; it necessitates a turning away from doomed replication. And what of history?
—William Least Heat-Moon, *Blue Highways*

Contents

Illustrations

Acknowledgments

IN ADDITION TO THANKING THE LITERARY JOURNAL *Spank the Carp*, who published an early incarnation of the monster-carp chapter, I'd like to thank everyone involved in this monsterquest—from the editors, board members, and staff at the University of Nebraska Press (particularly Matt Bokovoy, Heather Stauffer, Rosemary Sekora, Sara Springsteen, and Kyle Simonsen) to the guides and specialists I worked with in the field (especially Drew Price, Captain John Krol, Fabrizio Terenghi, and Luca De Prezzi) to all the suppliers of images who provided permissions. I'm grateful as well to the University of Central Arkansas for a research-based leave of absence that allowed for some relief from the monstrosities of academia, as well as the Marist College Florence campus, whose staff, administrators, teachers, and students provided lodging and fine company while I realized the last half of this book. None of this would have been possible, however, without support from the Estate of Nancy MacKenzie, whose foresight and fighting spirit will always serve as an example of how to live a life with purpose.

Thanks also to the Pirate's Alley Faulkner Society, who awarded an earlier version of this manuscript the honor of shortlist finalist in their 2017 William Faulkner–William Wisdom Narrative Nonfiction Competition.

Special acknowledgments to Scotty "Goggle Eye" Lewis for assistance with gar on the fly, Bill Wilmert for gar-fly-fishing guidance, Rob Watts for an insider look at Euro carp culture, Lee Merritt for helping a brother out, and Dr. Robert "Turkey Buzzard" Mauldin for translating the language of carbon calculations into layman's terms. Thanks also to my nephew River Rasmussen for being just as excited as me to reel in a dogfish, and über-angler Henry Hughes for invaluable fish knowledge and top-shelf editing advice. Special thanks as well to Thomas McGuane for inspiring a necessary, terrifying, and sobering introspection.

But mostly, I'd like to thank poet-scholar Lea Graham, who accompanied me on many of these expeditions, for being there and being who she is: an extremely fun traveling companion whose encouragement and perspective have added profound depths to the quality of this fisherman's existence. I'm lucky to have her in my life and as my wife, and I dedicate this book to her in the hope that this effort will create some converts to help preserve what we've got left.

IN SEARCH OF MONSTER FISH

I

Demythologizing Demonologies

Snakeheads and Piranhas Rabid in the Amazon

THIS WASN'T A TYPICAL FISHING TRIP. USUALLY I RESEARCH a fish, target a fish, seek out its authorities, make elaborate travel plans, then finagle support from my university if I can. But in this case, all I had was a larval idea. Given the huge amount of recent TV shows featuring "monster fish," such subject matter was obviously of interest to a mass audience, so therefore marketable. More importantly, this was stuff I'd been studying for over forty years—from catching big, old ugly lunkers to researching aspects of wildness in art history and literature to speaking on behalf of demonized grotesques. So I wasn't just thinking about investigating the eco-issues of some of the world's most terrifying fish, I was prepared to hop on that bandwagon and write my own monster-fish book.

Little did I know that as I started that first chapter, I was also starting a new chapter in a new life—in a place I'd never dreamed of going: the Amazon. Being the hugest river system in the world, four thousand miles long and over 150 miles across at the delta, the entire drainage basin covers 40 percent of South America. With more than 2,200 species of fish, the Amazon and its veins contain the vastest spectrum of fish on the planet.

But the thing was, I hadn't lit off to the Cuyabeno Wildlife Reserve on the equator to fish at all. The real reason I had gone was for both the most profound and dumbest of reasons that have ever existed: I was in love.

It wasn't even part of my plan to take my work to Ecuador. I'd flown to the Andes to be with her, and I'd put my workaholic ways on hold. Being a globe-trotting adventurous type, she'd taken me on an overnight bus ride followed by some roller-coaster taxi madness to a launch point on an artery of the Amazon where we were greeted by a photo on a restaurant wall of one of the most massive and impressive monster fish I had ever seen in my life. It was a twelve-foot-long arapaima caught by extreme angler Jakub Vágner, hauled from the very tributary we were setting out on.

Our guide from a local tribe, Wilson, picked us up, and we took off in a motorized canoe to our lodge amidst the anacondas. Somewhere in that river, there were three-hundred-pound piraiba catfish, and we saw all sorts of monkeys and sloths and parrots in the trees.

On the first of our four nights as the only gringos in our isolated neck of the woods, Wilson led us on a midnight hike with his trusty machete in hand. He was pointing out tarantulas and bizarre bugs and explaining strange animal calls. It was pitch black except for our flashlight beams as we wound through the rattle of bamboo rats and caimans blurping in the night. Then we came to a ferny marsh full of crazy orchids and hidden snakes.

The three of us were wearing rubber boots as Wilson led us further in, shining his light into the water. He then handed his machete to Lea, and I saw a sight so badass that it seared its image into every molecule of my being. The most gorgeous, fun-loving poetry professor that I had ever met in my life was raising a two-foot blade above her head, then bringing it down with a sudden swipe, right across the spine of a tilapia-looking fish lit up in the flashlight beam.

She, of course, had never done this before, and that fish, of course, had never been guillotined across its back. That machete, however, hit a log and stopped short, and the fish shot off, zigging and zagging to a palm frond floating in ankle-deep water. When I pulled back the leafy cover, it was nowhere to be seen.

Wilson had already bagged several of these fish in a plastic sack to convert into breakfast the next morning. He called them *dormelinas*, meaning "sleepy fish."

Anyway, we kept mucking on, until we came to another fish. It was long and skinny and covered with cheetah spots and treading in place. Wilson called it "Juan *chi chi*," which in Mexican Spanish translates to "Johnny tits." But in Ecuadorian Spanish, the meaning is more ambiguous. He handed the machete to me.

So I slashed Juan across the back. The blade went straight through its entire body and into the mud between my feet. A khaki-colored plume immediately clouded the water, and we waited for it to clear. It took a minute, and then I saw the silvery flash of its rolling back half. I scooped it up with my bare hand, and there was something familiar about its streamlined contours, especially its eely dorsal fin rippling from the shock of being severed completely in half.

Then I saw the front half spiraling on the edge of the cloud, so I grabbed it. Predictably, it chomped me a good one. And, I would add, with the speed and intensity of a viper hell-bent on getting in one last lunge—a feat it accomplished with bloody success.

Nevertheless, I pulled it from the swamp. In my hand, two fingers sliced open in three separate spots, I held the notorious snakehead, its fangs still snapping for more human flesh.

When snakeheads got loose in the United States right after 9/11, people freaked out. This happened on the heels of the anthrax attacks, when the country was as paranoid as a country could be. When a snakehead was found in a Maryland pond, the media rushed to that spot and continued to scream that the sky was falling—a sky full of man-eating apex predators waiting to devastate an entire continental ecosystem!

But it wasn't just Maryland where snakeheads were on the lam. They'd gotten loose in California, Florida, and Massachusetts. From 2002 to 2008, they were also found in North Carolina, Illinois, New York, Pennsylvania, Virginia, and Wisconsin. They even escaped from a fish farm in Lonoke, Arkansas, which is why I joined an extermination effort in

2009 that somehow escaped the radar of international news as the largest "fish purge" in world history. As in most previous eradication efforts, every living creature in every system where snakeheads were suspected of being was wiped out in order to eliminate a creature that apparently threatens citizens of this nation on the same level as radical Islamic jihad.

I went out with biology students from the University of Central Arkansas, and we used the chemical known as rotenone to deplete ditches of oxygen. Rotenone had already been used to treat forty-nine thousand watershed acres covering more than 440 miles of streams in the state. This highly coordinated effort involved agents from multiple wildlife agencies, ATVs, helicopters, and over a million dollars earmarked specifically for snakehead annihilation. But ultimately, only 150 snakeheads were eradicated from a much larger number still swimming around out there—a fact which has pretty much vanished from our consciousness like the antidote we purpled the waters with after wasting every tadpole, minnow, and water snake that just happened to be a casualty in that obsessive war.

As we're finding out, snakeheads aren't the boogeymen we've made them out to be. They're even proving to be a valuable sport fish right in the heart of the U.S. capital. As Andrew Zimmern showcased on a 2013 episode of *Bizarre Foods* filmed in Washington DC, these fish are now prey to bowhunters, and there's a place for snakeheads on American dinner tables.[1] And as we've seen in Arkansas and other places invaded by these nonnative species, this is no plague of biblical proportions. It's a bummer, of course, to have to deal with invasives, but keeping our fears in check is also advisable.

In the Ecuadorian Amazon snakeheads are just as much a presence as the parasitic candiru catfish, which are way scarier. These translucent little buggers, also known as "vampire fish," aren't much thicker than a toothpick, and they have a reputation for entering human genitals and digging in with barb-like fins to bloat themselves with blood. But for as long as our dread of this fish has been around, along with the knowledge that it can cause death or lead to castration, only one known case has ever been documented, and that wasn't until 1997.

The candiru cat has cousins that look like overgrown macaroni noodles that are equally as dangerous. These maggoty-looking fish are known for boring in and drilling through their hosts, Swiss-cheesing them to death. Just watch the 2014 "Amazon Apocalypse" episode of *River Monsters* to see how Jeremy Wade concludes that candirus & co., in collusion with piraiba and redtail catfish with a side of piranhas, devoured an overturned boatload of humans.[2]

But according to the website *Rainforest Expedition*, which echoes many other sources, the hype that surrounds the candiru is overblown. As the author states, "extensive research has indicated that much of this legend is probably a myth since Candirus detect the gills of fish by sight more than scent and the physics of fluid dynamics makes it impossible for them to swim up a stream of urine."[3]

But back to snakeheads: as it turns out, there is hardly any scientific literature on the role this fish plays in its natural ecosystems. Basically, the information we have is fear oriented, so if you can find anything on this species getting along with other species, which has been happening for more than 50 million years, then you're lucky. Almost every single Google search reveals that the brunt of what we know of this fish (which is also indigenous to Asia and Africa) decries them as aggressive, malevolent, air-breathing creatures that slither on land and attack humans. For the most part, this info comes straight from U.S. state agencies that want nothing to do with this fish, not foreign fisheries which don't see snakeheads as a problem.

Hence, data on wild snakehead populations coexisting with other species is virtually nonexistent. Still, there are a handful of articles by journalists who debunk the bloodthirsty reputation of this species, which made its pop culture debut in 2004 via the Lou Diamond Phillips horror movie *Frankenfish*, about mutant snakeheads in Louisiana devouring swimmers and fishermen.[4]

But according to an article published in *New Scientist*, snakeheads are oversensationalized tropical fish that cannot survive northern winters. Their hypothetical range of destruction is therefore limited. Editor Michael Le Page notes that a spokesperson for the Environment Agency in the United Kingdom claims that snakeheads are no more dangerous than pike. Le Page also asserts his disbelief of reports that accuse this fish of attacking humans.[5]

A Reuters article in the *Huffington Post* agrees with this observation, insisting that snakeheads "have gotten a bad rap." Fisheries biologist John Odenkirk is quoted as stating "intelligent management—not eradication" is the objective of the state of Virginia, where snakeheads "have not wreaked havoc with the Potomac River ecosystem."[6] Odenkirk's findings support those of Le Page, who concludes that "claims that it wipes out all other fish are just not true."[7]

We saw our first piranha two days later. Wilson took us into a backwater, rigged us up with some fresh-cut cane poles with six feet of heavy-duty monofilament then attached some homemade leaders fashioned from what looked like baling wire. He parked the canoe in the confluence of two streams and instructed us on what to do.

We baited up with chunks of beef that had been marinating in blood then thrashed our rod tips in the water, simulating an animal in distress. This is what attracts piranhas, which typically swim in schools of thirty to forty fish.

Within minutes Wilson pulled a bright orange, metallic-looking piranha into the boat. It glistened in the setting sun, dangling from his line. The upturned underjaw had highly visible triangular teeth, which is why *piranha* means "toothy fish" in the Tupi Indian language. And to show us what those pearly whites could do, Wilson gripped the fish in one hand, inserted a pencil-sized stick into its mouth with the other, and the piranha snapped it in half like an uncooked spaghetti noodle.

After a humid night filled with the revving roar of howler monkeys sounding like a stock car race, we found ourselves in the motorized canoe towing a primitive dugout up the Rio Cuyabeno. We went about two miles and entered a bayou in the smaller craft. With Wilson in the stern, Lea in the middle, and me up front, the three of us headed upstream, searching for manatees.

It was a hard paddle because the dugout weighed a couple hundred pounds, and the farther we traveled, the harder the current flowed. We were at the tail end of the rainy season, the water was up, and the flow was strong.

We went through a few lagoons, venturing deeper into territory that hadn't been traveled for months. Wilson kept breaking out his machete to chop branches blocking our path. And as the vegetation closed in, brushing our shoulders and heads, more and more bugs tumbled into the boat.

At one point something stung me, so I scooped some mud from the shallows and applied a poultice. This method had proved effective for Lea when something bit her the day before. I had chewed up a walnut and applied it to her bite, and it sucked the venom out. Whether the culprit be a biting fly or some sort of wasp, I've found that starchy substances like bread or chips can absorb toxins if you can get a moist mash on in time.

We were also constantly bailing with a radiator coolant jug because the dugout had a minor leak. Just an inch of water on the bottom of the boat added another hundred pounds, which could be felt in every stroke.

We traveled five miles, Wilson constantly hacking away. Sometimes we'd come to a fallen tree, then maneuver the boat under it and crawl over the branches. Other times, Wilson would chop straight through a one-foot-diameter log. His machete proved to be much more efficient than an axe or saw, and we eventually made it to a spot where he cut some more cane and assembled our poles.

Tied to a tree, suspended in a deep spot where the current had some pull, we baited our lines and thrashed our rods in the water. Minutes later, we felt them on the other end. It was a lot like fishing for sunnies, but getting piranhas to connect was tougher. When teeth like those start tearing on a piece of meat, it doesn't take long for the bait to get shredded off the hook. Plus, I'm sure they could sense the metal, and there's a certain art to setting the hook. But if you set the hook with too much enthusiasm, you risk launching a piranha out of the water and into

1. Spitzer and piranha. Photo by Lea Graham.

the boat. When that happens, it will snap away maniacally because that's its main defense. And if a piranha is off the hook and in your boat, then you better watch out for any exposed toes, especially if there's water in the hull for it to shoot around in.

I caught the first one. It was a white piranha about ten inches long and silvery with sparkles. It had swallowed the hook, so I passed it back to Wilson, who got it out. After that, he gutted it and used the organs as chum. We watched the swim bladder floating downstream. Within minutes the cannibals arose, devouring it and making the surface boil— but nothing like in the movies.

Since the little guys kept jacking our bait, we moved on to another spot, fishing in the blazing sun. Lea and I were dripping with insect repellent, sunblock, and sweat, but Wilson seemed as dry as the ludicrous, luminous, ornate blooms flowering vibrantly from the lush.

Meanwhile, Lea was becoming increasingly incensed at the punks that kept swiping her bait. The more her curses increased, the more I saw how she was taking this challenge seriously. Her invectives were aimed directly at the fish, who she addressed with colorful language, which never failed to crack me up.

By midafternoon I caught another, but this one was just a little sucker, not more than six inches. I threw it back, and then Wilson caught another.

The sun was now high in the sky, and since we were burnt out on fishing, we ate some pastries Wilson brought along. They were ball-shaped pancakes with chunks of bananas stashed inside. Wilson called them "hidden love" (that's the translation), and then we had a plantain or two.

Sitting there eating lunch, I began to wonder what would happen if any of us fell in. I'd learned from fishing shows that piranhas rarely attack humans, but on the other hand, I'd seen what the thrashing of our cane poles could do, and I'd seen how they had swarmed the swim bladder. This was definitely something I needed to look into.

The first nasty rumors about piranhas going postal were actually popularized by a populist American President. In his memoir *Through the Brazilian Wilderness*, Theodore Roosevelt described the species as a "cannibal fish . . . that eats men when it can get the chance." Roosevelt clearly relished expressing his biased opinion and went to great lengths to pigeonhole this fish as dangerous and aggressive. As he went on to explain:

> They are the most ferocious fish in the world. Even the most formidable fish, the sharks or the barracudas, usually attack things smaller than themselves. But the piranhas habitually attack things much larger than themselves. They will snap a finger off a hand incautiously trailed in the water; they mutilate swimmers . . . they will rend and devour alive any wounded man or beast; for blood in the water excites them

to madness. They will tear wounded wild fowl to pieces; and bite off the tails of big fish. . . . Most predatory fish are long and slim, like the alligator-gar and pickerel. But the piranha is a short, deep-bodied fish, with a blunt face and a heavily undershot or projecting lower jaw which gapes widely. The razor-edged teeth are wedge-shaped like a shark's, and the jaw muscles possess great power. The rabid, furious snaps drive the teeth through flesh and bone. The head with its short muzzle, staring malignant eyes, and gaping, cruelly armed jaws, is the embodiment of evil ferocity.[8]

Roosevelt continues his narrative, describing multiple "exhibition[s] of such impotent, savage fury" by these "pests of the waters." He then follows this with stories of folks being dismembered if not devoured. There's even a tale about a guy getting his tongue bit off, and another of a dead man discovered in a fjord, "his clothes uninjured but every particle of flesh stripped from his bones." Piranhas are then described as "a veritable scourge in the waters they frequent," "blood-crazy fish," and "ferocious little monsters."[9] It should be noted, however, that the brunt of support for these arguments comes from second- or third-hand stories that Roosevelt didn't even witness—which is how fish stories happen.

According to the *National Geographic* website, "In a historic visit to Brazil, Theodore Roosevelt famously saw a group of piranhas shredding pieces of a cow carcass in seconds," but this is not true at all. Roosevelt actually contradicted that information, stating that "If cattle are driven into, or of their own accord enter, the water, they are commonly not molested." But whatever the case, *Nat Geo* makes the point that Roosevelt's "dramatic account would color popular imagination for years, even though it was based on a manipulated spectacle in which fishermen blocked off a group of the fish and starved them beforehand."[10]

Point being, according to the BBC, "The piranha's reputation as a fearsome predator may not be fully deserved . . . experts from St. Andrews University say that piranhas are omnivores who mainly eat fish, plants and insects."[11] As for grouping up like a marauding biker gang, this article explains how they school to defend themselves with fish of

2. Piranhas frita. Photo by Mark Spitzer.

reproductive age positioned in the middle of the shoal. Nonetheless, the image of these fish as predators gone wild was tapped into by Hollywood, resulting in movies like *Piranha* and *Piranha 3DD*, the latter being an extremely sensationalist celebration of the B-genre horror flick with bouncing breasts and bloody fish bursting from the 3D screen—which is another way fish stories happen.[12]

What gets lost in this whole discussion are the possibilities that piranhas offer. For example, the *Houston Chronicle* reports that the flesh of this fish is "the cure for problems dealing with fertility, virility, even baldness." The article goes on to claim that "It is said to be the ultimate aphrodisiac." There's an account of a fisherman's father being sterile, but after eating piranha, he fathered three children. Similarly, "Maria Luisa Quepo, a childless woman near Pulcallpa, gave birth to twins when she was in her 40s after drinking a piranha-based brew."[13]

Still, the medical community doesn't seem to have any literature on the health benefits of piranha meat. There also seems to be a debate as to whether the taste is bitter or not—which led to my next question.

While traveling in Thailand a few years back, I was told that snakehead was commonly used in a horrible-tasting medicinal broth. I never got a chance to confirm this, but the snakehead that Wilson cooked was fried whole with its head on. Basically, it was greasy and unremarkable, unlike the one I'd grilled in Arkansas. That one was from Vietnam. I got it from an Asian market in Missouri and marinated it in a garlic chili peanut sauce. My guests and I found the meat to be firm and *sabrosa*, meaning "delicious." Verdict being: it's how you cook it.

As for the piranhas, Wilson fried them as well, serving them with limes on the side. Then came the moment of truth, where we would weigh claims of its bitter flesh versus Roosevelt's statement that piranhas are "fairly good to eat, although with too many bones."[14]

We cut into them, and the flesh was solid like a pork chop. The meat was white, and unlike chicken it wasn't stringy. If anything, the consistency and texture resembled gar, but it wasn't quite as rubbery. It was also quite sweet, nothing acrid about it whatsoever, and the bones were not an issue. Even more surprising, it had its own unique flavor.

It was mild but savory, almost even mushroomy, and buttery and juicy as hell. I even felt confident enough to state that it was "the most muy sabrosa" fish I'd ever eaten.

Lea agreed with that, but like I said before, this wasn't a typical fishing trip. And at that point, deep in the romantic Amazon where we'd been writing poetry to each other while waiting out the afternoon storms, anything and everything was admittedly overwhelming to us. Which is why I couldn't trust the idea of piranha meat being an aphrodisiac: because the whole experience was just that, both physically and mentally.

Being a Minnesota boy in the Ecuadorian jungle isn't something that happens every day, nor is being attacked by half a crazed snakehead, hauling in mythic piranhas, and getting a firsthand look at what makes these fish so monstrous in our communal vision. Because when you have fish as fangy and fantastic as snakeheads and piranhas swimming around with crocodiles and candiru catfish, there's just no stopping the drama. Apocrypha automatically happens—to the point that we end up with a grotesque bouillabaisse we can't fully trust. So we do what we always do, and perhaps that's what we do best: we speculate, tell stories, imagine the worst in ourselves, and apply those qualities to a niche of the ecosystem that actually provides balance.

This dichotomy, though, that tension between what we know and what we don't, is what attracts us to the idea of monster fish. We know they're there, we know what they're capable of, but what we really don't know are the accurate, finite details of their documented behaviors.

But that's enough demystification, because stripping fish of vicious context isn't always helpful. That is, we could analyze our fears away, but they'd just be replaced by something else. The fact is, we need nightmares and we need scapegoats to be who we are just as much as snakeheads and piranhas need us to believe that they're more dangerous than they really are. It's a defense mechanism for all parties, which serves to provide distance between us.

Because if we get too close, we might see them as they really are. And if we see them as they really are, we could encroach on them like we believe they encroach on to us—when the bottom line is that we can live together conflict-free as we have for centuries: humans, snakeheads, piranhas, and all the monsters we create to keep our imaginations as alive as they can possibly be.

That's what I thought, looking upriver, envisioning all the bends I couldn't yet see. I was confident that pointing out who the real monsters are was a cliché as old as language itself and rarely effective in creating change. So if I was serious about finding meaning in monster fish, then I'd need an angle that would make the quest worth a damn for people other than myself.

In that instant, however, chowing down on piranha for breakfast, my future wife smiling across the table from me, I had no clue what I was after. I figured that whatever it was, it would soon reveal itself like a fish just jumping into a boat, magically supplying itself for dinner.

Man, was I wrong about that.

2

Welsing for Colossals in Catfishalonia

A Hypothetical History

I CHOSE CATALONIA FOR MULTIPLE REASONS. FIRST, FOR ITS ten-foot-long monster catfish that took off like wildfire when they were introduced into the Ebro River in the seventies, and secondly, to get a fix on this region in Spain. I was also intrigued by the geographical connection between my family history and this fish. Back during the Inquisition, my ancestors fled Spain and settled in a place now known as Spitz-on-the-Danube, where they became Spitzers. It's also where a fish known as the "Danube catfish" swam through the Austrian city of Wels, and eventually became known as the wels catfish.

All that aside, these truly massive cats, which are the largest freshwater fish in Europe, have established themselves from the United Kingdom to Uzbekistan, throughout half the EU countries, the Baltics, the Middle East, Russia, and parts of Asia. As an introduced species, this fierce and fugly fish is faring well throughout the world, such that the wels (aka *Silurus glanus*, European catfish, sheatfish, som, malle, or weller) has become a top predator almost everywhere it's been introduced as a world-class sport fish.

A freak 280-pounder was recently landed on the Po River in Italy by professional angler Dino Ferrari. Or, as the website *BroBible* framed it, "Italian Bro Wearing NASCAR Gear Catches Catfish Big Enough to

3. Viral image of Dino Ferrari and wels catfish. Courtesy of Dino Ferrari.

Swallow Ricky Bobby."[1] But the wels, as a species, has definitely thrived more dramatically on the Ebro in Spain. On the upper part there's a shore-angling industry of fishing with halibut pellets, but on the lower, it's more from boats. And since the best seafood would be closest to the coast, and since the fishing guide website that attracted me the most featured pictures of a nine-foot-long two-hundred-pounder caught from a craft called *Pussy Galore*, Fate had basically made its call. So I booked the trip, shot off, met Lea in Barcelona, and not too long after that, we were on the water.

Reports of sixteen-foot, man-eating catfish have been circulating in Europe since the Middle Ages. A hand and two rings were found in a wels in 1558, and a Hungarian child was allegedly eaten by one in 1613. The corpse of a seven-year-old was supposedly found in a catfish esophagus in 1754, and there's a report from Turkey about two teenage

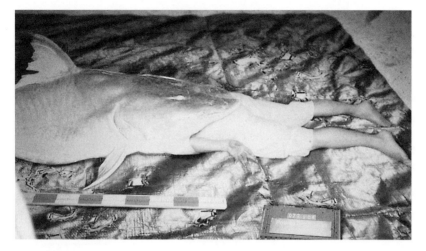

4. Widely circulated "man-eating" catfish image. Courtesy of Mark Spitzer.

girls being devoured by a *siluro* in 1773. These stories may just be rumors, or it's been posited that the accused river monsters might've recycled some drowning victims. Whatever the case, an 1853 article in *Fraser's Magazine* claimed two boys had been eaten by a massive wels. This article, written by an anonymous author, also pumped the hand story up to three rings.[2]

Such accounts are just as unverified as those of alligator gars attacking humans. What we can verify is that wels have been historically recorded at lengths of sixteen feet, and that they might be able to swallow children, but it's very unlikely that they could actually gulp down adults. There's a popular internet image of an alleged five-hundred-pound piraiba, an Amazonian cousin of the wels, that choked on a fisherman. What this indicates, if anything, is that a wels would have to be extremely enormous to eat a full-grown person, because that piraiba wasn't even big enough to get the job fully done. What it all comes down to is that we'd have to have some solid proof (not just hearsay) documenting a pattern of human-consuming behavior to confirm that these fish are actually "man-eating catfish."

Still, the wels can be aggressive, especially when guarding its brood. In 2008 a German bather was attacked in Lake Waidsee in Berlin and

17

suffered a seventeen-centimeter bite. Authorities estimate the size of this catfish to be not much more than three feet long, so imagine the damage a sixteen-footer could do.

Lately, though, the wels has made prime time in relation to one of the world's most debated crypto-creatures. Steve Feltham, a "Loch Ness Monster hunter" in Scotland, stated that after searching the legendary lake for twenty-five years, he'd come to the conclusion that Nessie was a misidentified wels. This offhand comment was picked up by Fox News and other entertainment venues that ran deceptive headlines insisting that the Loch Ness Monster was most likely a giant catfish.[3] Following that, similar headlines began popping up everywhere, spreading a type of news that isn't news at all. Unless, that is, tabloid news is news to you.

We pulled up to a chicken processing plant where a pipe full of blood and viscera was pumping out a pukey pink cloud of liquid stank, which was attracting minnows, which were attracting gulls. Tying up to that pipe, our guide threw out a cast net for live bait, which, he explained, wasn't quite legal on this stretch of the Ebro. He said that "the stupid city government" didn't encourage fishing for these cats and that live bait had been banned, except for worms, which are live bait. Hence, his conclusion that this law must've been up made by a woman. "Because," he noted, "whoever wrote it just doesn't understand that big fish eat smaller fish!"

Anyway, he pulled in some silvery three- and four-pound mullets, and we kept our mouths shut because he was the captain. The mullets were then rigged up to our hundred-pound braided lines, which were connected to hundred-pound fluorocarbon leaders, which were tied to steel leaders dangling beneath three giant, fluorescent, ice-cream-cone-shaped floats. Without question, these were the largest baits I'd ever fished with.

In the meantime, the wind was blowing, and this wasn't helping us. As our guide noted, the wels bite less when there's wind. He reasoned that waves create sound on the surface, and since these fish are extremely efficient hearers, noise can get in the way of prey. But as he also informed us, the bite usually picks up when the sun starts going down and the

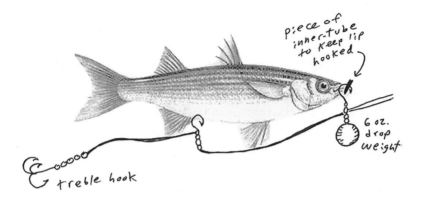

5. Mullet rig for wels catfish. Illustration by Mark Spitzer.

day starts cooling off. At that point, the wind lessens, and that's when his clients tend to get their cats.

It was nice, however, to have a breeze, because the day began baking away. It was 100 degrees in the broasting sun, and the three of us were sweating up a storm as our mullets tooled all over the place. The boat was anchored, and we had to keep switching our two-meter-long catfish poles around so that our floats could pass under the various lines. It was a bit like a shell game, and it took a lot of proactive action to keep from getting tangled.

We fished there for a couple hours, saw a couple huge cat backs breach, then moved upstream to a medieval-modern mashup of a town where ramparts and solar panels competed with steeples and smokestacks to define the skyline. It was a strange amalgamation of the old and the new, which is happening everywhere but not always so visibly.

We began drift-fishing by dragging a drogue, a parachute-looking canvas sack that slows the boat as it's pushed by the wind. This lessened the need to keep shifting our poles because now we were towing our bait. Nevertheless, the wind kept blowing, and the sun kept roasting with a ruthless desert heat.

By late afternoon I was nodding off, and by five o'clock it hadn't let up. By six o'clock it was even hotter. Then the wind died down.

That's when I started taking notes for my "defeat section," and that's when the orange float starting acting erratic because something was wigging out our largest mullet. Then that float, it shot off. But then it stopped.

The catfish had dropped the bait, but it was possible that it might circle back. Our guide told me to wait, so I stood poised, ready to hit the lever forward, lock the spool, and set the hook.

Suddenly, the float shot off like a rocket, the guide gave the signal, and I hauled back with brute force. The rod arced. It took less than a second to know that something was on, and it was mongo.

An epic battle then ensued, hauling back and leaning forward, cranking cranking cranking in line. That big old Penn baitcasting reel was bringing in the fish, and the boat was spinning. Lea and the guide were scrambling to reel in the other lines as I horsed and horsed that mother in for about fifteen minutes.

When we saw the orange flash of the float below, I knew a monster was coming up. Its eely form began slashing into sight, and when we saw it, Lea gasped. It was the six-foot wels I'd come to get, and it was on like Donkey Kong!

I got it up next to the boat, and the first thing I noticed was the stunning speckled pattern on its sides. It was a gold-and-black mosaic that reminded me of Gustav Klimt's *The Kiss*, a painting that also goes back to my Austrian heritage as well as the house I grew up in, where we had a print on the wall. And now that pattern was flashing on a leviathan that weighed at least a hundred pounds.

But that wasn't all in the color department because the skin around its pugnacious lower jaw and maw was a brilliant, electric saffron. And when it opened up that mega-mouth to regurgitate a half-digested European eel (and you would too if you'd been hauled up like that), I saw the same vivid coloration in the depths of its gorge.

The treble hook was lodged in one side of its mouth, and there was an injury on the other side: an angry red hamburger mass of shredded-up muscle and meat where it had been hooked before and not that long ago.

Our guide was gloved, and he grabbed the creature's mouth, which

6. Spitzer and Lea with wels. Courtesy of Lea Graham.

was lined with compact rows of stubby but needly teeth. That catfish's piehole was large enough to swallow a schnauzer, and it thrashed and got away from the guide. I reeled it back, and he got another grip on it, then hauled it over the rail.

That wels weighed 118 pounds, but we didn't have a tape measure. Still, we compared it to an iron bar on board, which I later used to calculate length. It was six-foot-three, one of the most enormous fish I'd ever caught.

Then we got the money shot, its semi-comic tiny tail flopping over the port rail, its super-wide frogzilla mouth glurping at the sky from the starboard side. Its six long whiskers were dangling down, and it had these teeny-weeny beady eyes that weren't much larger than BBs staring up from its flattened head. It just sat in my arms with its bulging gut, a gentle giant, who, it seemed, had been in this situation before so knew how to remain composed. Then I released it back to the Ebro, slipping and sliming over the rail, leaving me with an incredibly mucousy layer of goo coating my stomach and pants.

The second day, with Lea gone off hiking to a neighboring town, I didn't catch squat. Just spent eight torrid hours in the maddening sun. Why no fish hit, I don't know. That's the way it goes sometimes.

At night, Lea and I hoofed into the village where we'd gone the evening before. In the town square we'd discovered a friendly bar that made its own wine and offered a selection of local cuisine. Neither of us spoke or read Catalan, but I recognized the word *anguilla* on the menu, which I remembered from my eel studies. We ordered a plate of that, plus calamari and some sort of oxtail dish. Whereas the eel was exotic in a spicy sauce (small soft bones, cooked with the skin on), the fried squid was exquisite and the best we'd ever had. All we put on it was fresh-squeezed lemon juice.

It was *festa* time in this ancient place, meaning fireworks and live bands at night as well as loudspeakers pumping out Bruce Springsteen and Michael Jackson. This evening, however, was reserved for the running of the bull—which doesn't run wild through the streets anymore because things have changed due to a combination of political pressures and animal rights activism. Plus, it's not uncommon for folks to get maimed or killed when the bulls run. Nowadays, in many towns throughout Spain, the bulls are tethered to a gigantic firehose-looking strap, which is what this bull was strung to. It was controlled by at least twenty shirtless dudes who ran alongside it with hundreds of others: teenage girls, little kids, moms, dads, pastry makers, pretty much half the town.

This was part of an annual ritual that had survived and evolved just like the wels. Whereas the range of this fish had greatly expanded, the size of these cats has radically decreased. Be this due to overfishing or less feeder fish in the systems, I figured that if this trend continues we should count ourselves lucky to experience these fish in such mammoth form when they probably won't reach such lengths in another few generations.

Because that's what happens with fish; the more they get fished, the more their overall size diminishes. We can draw an analogy to the white sturgeon, which used to grow to twenty feet. But now, as the Audubon Society asserts, the white sturgeon maxes out at twelve foot six.[4] Accordingly, the largest wels on record measured 16.4 feet and weighed over 880 pounds, but these days, it's rarely half the length it used to reach. If you catch a 200-pounder, or one over 9 feet, that's about as big as they get.

Whatever the case, the past was apparent everywhere we went in that old stone village, but especially in that snorting bull charging across the cobblestones as we made our way back to the town square. Where, once again, we took advantage of Catalonia's historic cuisine existing in the modern age. We ate meatballs and garlicky squid, enjoyed tender duck in a glazy sauce, and indulged again in the best damn calamari the universe had to offer.

And as we sat there drinking chilled red wine in the humid night, I couldn't help romanticizing that as evolution continues to evolve, and as the past endures into the present, and as certain traditions persevere while others naturally die out, the remnants of a family colossus lurk in the murk of history.

The third day, back on the river, which was bordered on both sides by great brakes of cane, Lea came along. The joke was that she'd bring us good luck like she had the first day.

It had rained the night before, which was a good sign. Our guide said that if the river turned a chocolaty brown, then the bite would be on. Since wels catfish rely on their sense of smell and hearing and touch (via whiskers) to detect prey, they have an advantage over fish that rely on sight when the water is muddy.

But since it hadn't rained that much upstream, the water was as clear as the day before. In fact, it was so clear that you could see labyrinths of Eurasian milfoil growing thick throughout the system. In the United States this plant life is invasive, and state agencies are fighting it like a pox that takes over entire lakes, crowding out all life. But in Europe, *Myriophyllum spicatum* is a native vegetation that's not as threatening.

We took off later than usual since we were planning to stay out into the evening, shooting for the windlessness. Motoring upstream, we caught more contraband mullets, then sweltered in the blazing sun.

The hours went by, but it was cooler than the day before, and cooler than the day before that. The wind riffled throughout the afternoon, and we saw plenty of gulls and blue herons, plus another model of a smaller heron with a checkery pattern and a slightly different coloration. The cattle egrets were basically the same as those in the states.

Then, around seven o'clock, just like two days before, that orange float went straight down.

"Strike!" the guide yelled.

I jumped up, locked the lever, and hauled back as hard as I could. Fish on!

"Can you bring in that other float?" I asked Lea, who jumped to the task and started reeling. I wanted to get the other lines out of the way. Not only that, I wanted to give her a crack at this fish. But I knew she'd need the fighting belt to keep the butt of the rod from digging into her pelvis—which I didn't need because I was wearing a leather belt.

"Can we get the fighting belt out?" I asked our guide, but his response was something I didn't expect.

"NO!" he shouted, not at me but at Lea. "Leave that float out there! Leave them all out there! Another fish might come along!"

So she left it out as he ordered, and I battled a wels that felt a lot lighter than the one I'd caught two days before. Yet sometimes it would surge, and when that happened, I questioned my assessment.

This one came in a lot quicker. Lea declined to fight it, so I battled it for about five more minutes, and then it was beneath the boat. Predictably, it was tangled in the line that the guide told Lea to leave out. She was shooting video (see "Spitzer vs. Wels Catfish" on YouTube), and he started flipping out.[5]

"No!" he scolded. "This is not the time for video! Put that down and hand me that pole! We've got to get this mess untangled, or we'll lose the fish!"

Meanwhile, I was fighting a monster cat that was testing everything I had. My pole was bending, and the other line was wrapped around my line right beneath the tip of the rod. This got our guide up on the bow, where he tried to reverse the knotted mess. Lea had to let out line from the other reel and give him some slack to work with so that the other line wouldn't slice through mine. Basically, our huffing, puffing guide was trying to create a loop to pass an entire fishing pole through, and the fish was giving him guff.

He began shouting orders at me like, "Step back!" and, "Give me some room to operate!" when I was the guy fighting the fish—a procedure we went through several times when he should've just cut the other line and hauled the tackle in by hand.

Anyhow, he worked on getting the mess unraveled while I held the fish a foot beneath the boat, where I was trying not to yank it or spook it or make it run in any way. Because if it lurched, the rod could slam down on the rail and break. Even worse, it could lasso one of his fingers and sever it right off.

But then we were free, and I brought it up: a long, dark, even eelier-looking wels. Whereas the first one had been a technicolored neon fatty, this sinewy overgrown sperm of a fish was black and white in coloration. Its tapering anal fin was rippling away, the whole fish looking at least five feet long. But ultimately, after we hauled it in, it turned out to be an inch shy of seven feet and 123 pounds!

It was a male fish, according to our guide, who noted its funny little vestigial dorsal. He also pointed out the pointy shape behind its vent. The females, he said, had a more thumb-shaped flap of skin in that spot.

Again we took a round of pictures, and as we did, our guide pulled its jaws apart so we could get some shots of its throat. Past some of the most impressively menacing, fancy-looking gillworks I had ever seen, you could see four sandpapery crushing pads. Because what these catfish do is they grab their prey with their up-front teeth, then literally Hoover their food straight back, where those pads smash down with hundreds of pounds of pressure and crush stuff to smithereens.

Like the other catfish, we released this one, as is the norm. And the second after it vanished into the Ebro, the silence was totally palpable. It had been a great fish and a bigger fish, but to paraphrase Hunter S. Thompson's suicide letter . . . football season was over.[6]

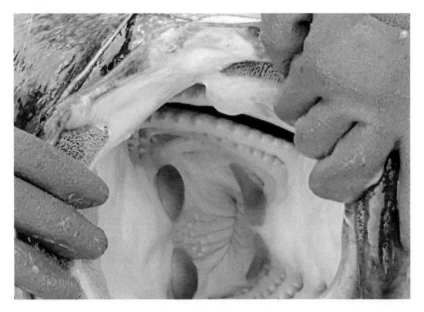

7. The maw of the beast. Photo by Lea Graham.

One thing I should mention is the pool. We had this really cool, above-ground swimming pool—and by "cool" I mean *imperative when it's 100 degrees*. It was outside the guest quarters where clients stayed. It was a trailer and it wasn't that big, but it was comfortable enough. It had two bedrooms, a sitting area, a kitchenette, and a fan.

So Lea and I, we'd come back from fishing, and we'd get a beer, and we'd get in that pool, and that pool made all the difference. In that pool we had quite a few heavy-duty conversations. One went like this:

"It seems there's some illegality," she said, "in these fishing trips you take. I'm wondering how you deal with that."

"What do you mean?" I asked.

"Well, when we went piranha fishing in the Amazon, our guide was always looking out for the authorities because it wasn't legal to fish. But that's what happens. All the guides were doing that, and all the tourists were doing that. It's part of the experience. And now, over here, we find that it's not legal to fish for wels with live bait, but as our guide told us, the other guides do it too. He asked us not to take pictures of the bait, and he asked you not to mention them in what you write. How do you deal with that?"

I'd been thinking about this for a while, and I'd also been researching why live bait was illegal on the Ebro. An email to the Pesca Continental division of the Catalonian government had come back with the reply that live bait was banned "as a method of control and eradication of invasive species."[7] The Google translation was awkward, but it echoed a document I found online published by the Aragon region upstream, which stated, "In order to avoid further spread and invasion of non-native species potentially harmful to aquatic ecosystems and the species that inhabit them, the use as bait of live, dead, parts or derivatives of any specimen of any species of fish, except dead sardines" is prohibited.[8] Meaning that because there are now twenty-two invasive fish species in all Catalan river systems as compared to thirty indigenous fish species, the Spanish government wasn't taking any chances.[9] Thus, the situation was akin to a country like the United States banning anyone from coming in, whether they be foreigners or citizens, just to keep out Mexicans.

But back to the original question, which had to do with what I chose to address in relation to what I chose not to mention. "I work with a lot of guides," I responded, "and they all have certain demeanors. I once worked with a famous guide who called black people 'crack monkeys,' and I once worked with another who constantly referred to women as 'bitches.' These instances are rare, and more times than not my guides are fine people. But for those who have issues, I suspect it has something to do with knowing fish better than humans—which is why they tend to get the fish for me. And when they do, I don't complain. That's what I pay them for, not their anecdotal insights or company. When it comes to writing about fishing, it should be about fishing. Or mostly about fishing."

I then rambled on about how I'd tried to discipline myself into sticking to the subject matter when tension exists between telling the story as a journalist (which I am, in a way, when I write about fish) and telling the story in a literary way for university presses that don't wish to raise any hackles. For them, it doesn't make commercial sense to venture into areas where controversial views can complicate things.

This brought me back to our purposely unidentified catfishing guide, who knew his stuff and produced the fish. But sometimes his anger boiled over. He once snapped at me like he snapped at Lea, and it had been over nothing. I'd been putting mullets into a tub, and he yelled at me because I wasn't holding the lid over it and he thought some might jump out. But so what if they did? He'd just catch more.

There were a number of other things he'd said that were also disturbing. He'd definitely been critical of some Arabs we saw at the launch one day, and he told me that it's idiotic to put terrorists on trial when videotapes show them chopping off heads. His thesis was that they should just be executed.

That's not to say that this guy was all bad. I did have some good conversations with him about gun control and the dilemma of the Confederate flag, in which we seemed to be on the same page. But when a boat got too close to us on the river, or someone was parked on the ramp when we came in, some anger management issues arose.

"Well," I went on, still trying to address her question, "I try not to get personal, and I sometimes have to censor myself, or what I want to write about. But in this case, I think I need to be honest about the bait we used and how we got it. Not that it's a big deal, but my loyalty is to history, not him."

"What do you mean?" Lea asked.

"What I mean is, I need to be faithful to the details that matter, not his business interests. I never agreed to leave anything out."

But then I got even more abstract, taking the stance: "This is a history. That is, what I'm investigating . . . it's a history of a fishery, but it's also a history of a bunch of histories clashing and reacting and searching for balance. Some people love the wels over here, and others claim they're wrecking the food chain. But it's not just about catfish anymore because they're only part of the equation. And like all histories, there's no way to be completely objective. It's a hypothetical history."

This half-baked theory then led to a much more relevant observation, one that's key to what I kept trying to get at but just kept skirting. And it goes like this:

So Lea and I, we're sitting in that pool, and we each have our histories, and we're each checking to see if our histories are compatible, and the subject is how ecosystems change because of change. Because of migration. Because of native species and nonnative species moving around like humans do—due to all the expulsions and migrations and genocides and slaveries and mass-agricultural pressures on the planet, plus all the jobs and wars and politics that just keep getting repeated.

And Lea—radiant, smiling—says, "You know, getting a close look at those fish really gives you a sense of history."

And she hits the nail right on the head, informing me with certainty that I couldn't have said it any better.

And this insight, it supplies what I need to end the chapter with finality—even though I still have questions. The main one being: where is all this monster stuff going, and where will it take me next?

3

Cuda Chaos in the Dominican Republic

Only Beaten by the Waves

AFTER PROPOSING IN OLD STONE SANTA DOMINGO IN A fortress mortared with animal blood (she said yes and loves the ring), then whale watching in Samaná, we shot off for the white-sand beaches of Bayahibe. Why? Because the next fish on my bucket list was the infamous barracuda, a tropical top predator renowned for attacking humans and devouring prey with torpedo-like velocity. I'd been jonesing to fish for this species for years, so now my mission was to investigate its legendary aggressiveness to see if its reputation had been rightly earned as a truly ferocious monster fish.

But if the barracuda has a worldwide range, why this island in the Caribbean with Haiti on the other side? Well, it was a place I knew nothing about, with a culture I knew nothing about, which attracted me. Plus, Lea had lived in the Dominican Republic back in graduate school, and she also knew Spanish and how to get around. More importantly, she was my favorite person on the planet, and I couldn't get enough of her. And since she, like me, loved going out on the water, that's what we decided to do.

We met our contact from the guide service at Bayahibe Fishing Centre at eight in the morning, and she took us down the beach where we boarded a twenty-foot fiberglass boat. It had a forty-horse Yamaha, a shade canopy, and a live well with holes drilled right through the hull that allowed for aeration.

Our guaranteed "English-speaking" guide didn't speak any English at all, but Eduardo had a silent confidence that was reassuring and agreeable. He motored us out of the marina and into the amazingly greenish turquoise waters calicoed with a blacker blue and put the hammer down. The bow lifted, we began planing, and three seconds later the engine died.

Lea and I shared a wary stare as Eduardo opened the cowl and began banging on something with a rusty chunk of rebar. That's when I noticed that the drain cork was wrapped in a plastic bag just like the lid of the gas tank to provide a tighter seal. As for the rinky-dink linkages inside the outboard, they were held together with snarls of wire as Eduardo rigged up a length of heavy-duty line, which he wound around the throttle handle. It was a jimmy-rigged solution which kept coming undone for the rest of the day, but hey, that's the type of innovation found in developing countries that aspire to evolve into "middle-income" countries. The Dominican Republic, by the way, is supposedly the "world's happiest country" behind Costa Rica.[1]

So off we went—past bright-white diving gulls, low-soaring *pelicanos*, and crucifix-looking frigate birds kiting in the sky—to a spot where Eduardo slowed down and broke out two six-foot fluorocarbon leaders with three rubber squid lures on each, which he attached to two huge fishing rigs. The six-foot trolling rods were stout and stiff and pretty much solid steel. They were equipped with jumbo baitcasting reels—one the size of a mayonnaise jar, the other the size of a coffee can. The line was at least one-hundred-pound test, and each rod and reel weighed about forty pounds. Eduardo positioned them in their holders on opposite sides of the boat and let out about fifty yards on both.

Within minutes, a rod tip started nodding. Eduardo motioned for me to reel in, so I locked the spool and began cranking. There was no resistance at all, and I could see a small silvery fish flopping on top of our wake. When we got it in the boat, it looked like a mini tuna. Eduardo unhooked it, said it was a *cojinua*, and threw it in the live well.

Not too long after that, trolling along the mangrovey roots of Isla Saona, Lea reeled in a stripy green-and-yellow fish with a flattened, toady head, its wide froggy mouth serrated with tiny fangs. It was about ten inches long, and Eduardo called it *la rajula* and threw it in the live well. It was a fish I later failed to identify, but with thousands of crazy-colored, bizarre-looking species down there, this was to be expected.

Since we now had enough bait, it was time to change locations. Eduardo shot out into the wind, and we began smack-smack-smacking on the chop. It was a rough ride, but hardly as rough as what was to come.

There are twenty-eight recognized species from the taxonomy *Sphyraena* (meaning "pike-like"), which goes back 50 million years. The smallest members are just a few inches long, and the largest members are reported to grow to nearly two meters. Seaworld claims barracuda can reach lengths of three meters, even though the official world record is just under seven feet.[2] That 102.5-pound Guinean barracuda was caught in the Cuanza River in Angola. The largest great barracuda, on the other hand, is listed as weighing 103 pounds and measuring five and a half feet long.[3]

According to the Florida Museum of Natural History, barracuda can reach speeds of over thirty-six miles per hour. These opportunistic feeders are also served by "binocular vision," meaning they see straight ahead and rely mainly on sight in the day for taking down prey. This function, coupled with a highly muscular aquadynamic body structure, allows them to strike like lightning. Hence, there are very few predators capable of doing a cuda in. Humans aside, killer whales, giant tunas, sharks, goliath groupers, dolphins, and cannibalistic barracuda are pretty much the only creatures with the huevos to even try.

Barracuda are also known for biting fish in half and taking down fish larger than themselves. For centuries, humans have reportedly been on their à la carte menu. Most incidents involve shiny objects which are mistaken for silvery fish. Other reports are connected with the flash of knives, or spearfishing, or provocation of some sort.

The Frost Museum of Science states, "The teeth of the great bar-racuda are sharp and can easily lacerate a human limb. Many attacks on humans . . . [end] in the loss of an arm or a leg."[4] This information, however, should be treated with a certain amount of skepticism. As the website MarineBio notes, "The great barracuda very rarely attacks humans."[5] And as the article "Debunking the Myths Behind Barracuda" asserts, "there have only been 25 documented and confirmed barra-cuda attacks in the last century, which is a negligible number when compared with other predators."[6] The Florida Museum of Natural History echoes this statement with the information that "such attacks are uncommon and more often than not easily preventable with a few simple precautions."[7]

Barracuda are also famous for flamboyant acrobatics. There's this video on YouTube titled "40 LB BARACUDA JUMPS INTO FISHING BOAT!!!" in which a guy is reeling one in and doesn't notice it leap. It blasts fifteen feet through the air, seemingly driving itself harder and faster through the realm of oxygen by shuddering every molecule of its body. The guy sees this in the last split second and leans slightly to the left, the fish missile just missing his face. It lands in the boat and thrashes around like an exorcism demon child.[8]

This is where the idea of the barracuda tornado comes in. This species has a tendency to clump up in "wolf packs" that rotate dramatically, the smaller fish on the inside protected by the larger ones. I've seen quite a few photos and videos of this slowly revolving phenomenon, which sometimes includes hundreds of fish. It's a bone-chilling sight, one that daring divers aspire to witness from the center of a whirling vortex that others fear could—like so many real tornadoes—suddenly start charting its own wild course.

Anyway, hold that thought, which we'll return to in due time.

The ride to the reef was brutal on the butt, jumping waves and slam-ming down. With the bow up high and the drain plug out, the live well behind our seat was a foaming volcano that kept erupting on our backs.

Passing some egrets and tricolored herons, we finally made it to the

8. Barracuda tornado. Photo © Andamanse, Dreamstime.com.

place: a vast expanse of underwater rocks and plants, but mostly just sand about three feet beneath the surface. I'd never understood the concepts of "flats" in literature dealing with tarpon and bonefish, but now I understood it well.

The area was protected by a ridge of coral that had claimed two rusted fishing boats both now set at catawampus angles. An archipelago of some small palm-treed islands also kept the waves at bay. So with the water now calmer and the occasional manta ray ghosting by, Eduardo rigged us up with bait—most of which consisted of some sardine-looking ballyhoos with their unicorn horns removed. A foot-long steel rod was skewered through each eight-inch fish, and a J-hook the size of a candy cane was attached where the rod emerged from the anus. The other end of that rod was attached to a steel leader, which was attached to a two-foot fluoro-leader, which was attached to the extremely thick mono-test spooled in the reel. Eduardo then let out line, trailing the bait on the surface.

We cruised around for over an hour, the sun rising higher in the sky. Nothing bit. Nothing happened. Eventually, Eduardo said they weren't biting.

That's when a rod jerked, but it was obvious that nothing was on. He reeled it in and the bottom half of the bait was gone, completely severed by razor-sharp teeth.

This was encouraging. I'd read that cudas frequently attack from behind, bite off the tail end, then come back to engulf the rest. In fact, the other rod then did the same, and when I reeled it in, we had another half-ballyhoo.

Eduardo put freshies on both rigs and let out line and circled back. It didn't take long for a rod to arc and start whizzing. When Eduardo signaled me to reel in, I jumped to the task. Again, there was no resistance at all. Just a strange silver slash breaking from our wake and cartwheeling across the surface. I reeled and reeled, and then it was under water and feeling like a gar. That is, being spear-shaped, it cut through the water with little resistance. It was just no match for that super rig—until we got it next to the boat. That's when I finally felt some tension. When its stripy back came into view, Eduardo grabbed the leader and yanked the fish into the air. It was about three feet long and seven pounds. Then suddenly it was in the boat and kicking up a fuss right between the three of us.

Lea actually screamed, which surprised me but surprised her even more. That's just not the way she rolls. When it comes to barracuda, though, it doesn't take much to imagine those choppers clamping onto an Achilles tendon, which is why she leapt away from its gnashing jaws. But to me, it seemed about as dangerous as any northern pike I'd ever landed, so I let it bang around and slap my shins.

Eduardo showed a bit more caution by conking it on the head. The concussion killed it, and he reversed the hook out of its bony upper palate.

Gripping the fish behind its head, I picked it up to examine it. It had two spiny dorsal fins and that prominent upturned lower jaw. The black blotches on its belly informed me that it was a great barracuda, and it had those trademark sharky fangs, some of them pointing backward to

9. Cuda mouth. Photo by Lea Graham.

prevent prey from escaping. The teeth have inner sheaths, or interlocking holes in the opposing jaws, but gazing into that maw, all I could see was the stuff of vampire movies.

"Be careful," Lea advised.

"No problem," I replied, and that's when it flexed and snapped. Sure, it was technically dead, but that didn't stop it from springing from my grip and landing between us.

Lea screamed again, leapt away once again, and again I apologized for freaking her out. I thought I'd had it under control, but as I found out, this was the fiercest, strongest, most unpredictable fish I had ever handled.

I wanted to get the trophy shot, so I grabbed it again, and again I assured her that I had control. But again, the same damn thing happened. It broke away, she screamed and leapt, and this time she was pissed. And so was I. I mean, this dead fish was messing with my credibility, and it was making my bride-to-be distrusting of me.

Eduardo told me to grip it from underneath, so I clenched the inner gills in my fist and there was no way in hell it could break loose. It tried, and I almost lost it, but I held on and kept control.

Meanwhile, the fact that Eduardo had brained this barracuda as a precautionary measure spoke to the fact that this fish's conservation status is highly stable, and it isn't endangered or vulnerable. According to the International Union for Conservation of Nature and Natural Resources (IUCN), the status of the great barracuda is that of "Least Concern."[9] Still, the specters of habitat loss, pollution, and sportfishing are something to consider. But this species' overall stability isn't just due to a dearth of its predators; another factor is that there's virtually no commercial industry for barracuda because of the dreaded ciguatera toxin. Since barracuda eat smaller fish, and because many of those fish process algae which are poisonous to humans, barracuda are often avoided as a food source. Symptoms of ciguatera food poisoning include gastronomical distress, weakness of limbs, and problems differentiating hot from cold. Basically, the literature states that any barracuda over ten pounds can bioaccumulate enough to become a carrier, so there's a wariness out there that acts as a defense mechanism and sustains populations.

I'd asked our contact at Bayahibe Fishing Centre if barracuda were safe to eat, and she had replied that she never takes that chance. This was the message I pretty much got from everyone and every source I consulted, so it bummed me out that Eduardo had iced this fish. I communicated to Lea that I'd like to release any more we caught, and she, in turn, translated that. Eduardo, however, responded that he would be glad to take it and any others we caught to feed to his family for Holy Week.

Then pow! It was Barracuda city! They were biting like crazy, and that's when all chaos broke loose. I hooked another three-footer, but this one was way huger. It leapt and ran and took out line, exploding

10. The big one. Photo by Lea Graham.

my mistaken perception that cuda can't fight. Then, when I finally got it in the boat, it went amok, somehow snapping Eduardo's finger and leaving a gash that's probably still in need of stitches. That fish weighed twenty pounds, and he dropped it in the live well.

Lea took the next one, but in handing her the rod I stepped on her foot, crushing her toes. Again she screamed but brought it in. It was the smallest of the bunch, only fifteen inches long, and Eduardo called it a *blanco*, meaning it was white. I couldn't see any difference in it, except that it lacked the dark belly splotches the other two had.

Then I lucked into a monster cuda. I didn't see it jump, but Eduardo got a gander at it and exclaimed that it was "Grande!" Figuring I'd set the hook, I hauled back hard on the rod and hit the canopy frame above, instantly snapping the line. Big mistake! I felt like a total dillrod after that and resolved not to set the hook again. If they were on, they were on, so no use taking any chances.

Eduardo was now trailing a handline to account for the pole I'd put out of commission. I hooked another fish, and in bringing it in I caught the handline, which ended up getting caught in the prop. Whatever the case, we landed that barracuda, another three-footer, this one nearly fifteen pounds, and eventually Eduardo untangled the mess.

"These fish are loco!" I cried, snagging a rock we thought was a fish. Eduardo directed me to reel in, so I locked the spool and the rod arced to the breaking point. We were in a jam, so I released the line and the bale spun at Mach speed. Another big mistake. The next thing we knew, we had a Medusa on our hands.

Eduardo began untangling that, the tiller swung freely on the transom, we drifted into some coral, and because he was uncoiling the bird's nest, the propeller began cracking and crunching with a gut-wrenching sound. Somehow, though, he got us out of there, and together we freed the line.

Following that, I got a twelve-pounder, another seven-pounder, lost a couple more, and then we were ready for lunch and snorkeling. Lea and I swam around, saw some cartoony-looking fish, then headed back with half a dozen barracuda. The chaos was over.

Or so I thought.

The next day, we were heading into the wind, and the weather had radically changed. The waves were whitecapping at three to five feet, and the hull was slamming down every few minutes with a skull-rattling intensity. Not only that, there were swells coming in beneath those waves, lifting them another six feet. Sometimes we'd go up, then suddenly plummet eight to ten feet.

I'd just told Lea that my study had changed from investigating rumors of the barracuda's violent nature to reflecting on the theme of chaos, which seemed to come stock with meeting these fish. I listed the litany of experiences we went through the day before as evidence of this, but now, as we were finding out, the chaos was much more than we'd bargained for. In fact, it was Chaos with a capital *C*.

Eduardo was standing in the stern expertly steering us up and down the crashing, smashing, cascading crests, and Lea and I were in the middle of the boat, our asses getting smacked by the bench seat every time the boat slammed down. It would've been nice to have had some life vests within reach (they were stowed in the bow), if not for the reassurance that if we flipped we might survive, then at least for the cushioning they could've provided our battered glutei maximi.

Then things got worse. The waves rose to seven feet, eight feet, and with all those swells, we were rising ten feet, twelve feet, thirteen feet, then bashing down with sledgehammer force. It even got to the point that I could feel my balls slapping the seat every time the keel smashed down. I sat on my baseball cap, and that lessened the thwack a degree or three.

Lea, in the meantime, was starting to get sick. She'd taken some seasickness pills earlier, but now her gut was surging like the pounding waves. She was clinging to the rail and looking pale.

We had an hour to go in an open boat on the open sea, and there was no protection from the wind in sight. In other words, we had to keep on pushing through the splashing, thrashing, kra-bashing fury of the relentless Caribbean because there wasn't any other choice.

"Isn't this dangerous?" Lea asked in Spanish, but Eduardo just shrugged. From the way he swayed and kept his footing, it was obvious that he was used to such conditions. But for us, we were entitled Americanos, so I felt indignant about having to pay for such discomfort. But more than that, it vexed me that my obsession had placed the love of my life in peril.

And for what? So I could write a monster-fish book? So I could continue to not catch what was still eluding me? I sure as hell wasn't getting any closer to anything—except death!

Then things got even worse. As we chugged to the top of a twenty-foot wave, I heard Lea gasp. It was looking like the little engine that could might not. The apex of the wave was curling above us and was about to come barreling down, but we made it by the hair of our chinny chin chins, the patched-up motor droning whenever it could find purchase, revving up and winding down according Eduardo's grip on this merciless sea that had already claimed countless lives.

And on it went, excruciating minute after excruciating minute, going more up and down than forward. And as it went on, surfing through gullies, gliding through gaps, more and more water slapped us in the face. Gallon after gallon, bucket after bucket, drenching us, in our eyes, stinging us! We were already totally soaked except for one cargo pocket of my shorts, the only dry spot on both our bodies. It was holding my notebook, which was filled with pages of water-soluble fishing notes I'd spent two days compiling. All it would take was one good hit and all the details I'd been collecting would be completely wiped out. Why this didn't happen I have no clue, because we were definitely being abused.

By the smash of the ocean! The bash of the sea! By the rising, the diving, the hell-pounding of the seat! Gastric acids bubbling! I couldn't take any more, had to stand up, get off my ass! So I lurched to my feet and grabbed the canopy, locked my legs, and turned my pocket away from the spray. And that did it. It was easy enough to just cling for dear life, white-knuckling the steely frame.

On and on we raged through the chaos. The chaos of cudas, the chaos of slaves! Torture, hurricanes, military might! Crashing and smashing over thousands of leagues of gone treasures, corroded cannons, the casualties of empires, pirates, prisoners, refugees! Lost histories riddled with rape, malaria, massacres, mass suicide—the whole horror of this gorgeous, genocidal, sun-blazoned place! Which, now, is also an all-exclusive destination for frequent flyers seeking golf-course-spa massages. But where are the Arawaks now? A quarter million wiped out in just two years! Thanks a lot, Christopher Columbus!

And there she was: my pretty, ailing fiancée—who I'd hauled off on a madman's quest—fighting the shock of her own intestines, sheets of spray smacking her face, being beaten like a dog. Still, as we both confirmed later on, we were consoled by the fact that at least we would die together.

But then, of course, we made it to the jetty. And as soon as we rounded it, we were out of the wind and coming in.

On the plane ride over, I'd been reading *Feast of the Goat* by Mario Vargas Llosa, a novel based on the Trujillo dictatorship that took its toll on millions of Dominicans. That book was filled with all sorts of murders and assassinations that had affected the political evolution of the DR in the twentieth century. One passage, though, that stuck out to me was from the protagonist's point of view in Santo Domingo: "She is at the corner of Independencia and Máximo Gómez in a crowd of men and women waiting to cross. Her nose registers a range of odors as great as the endless variety of noises hammering at her ears."[10] Noises that the author described in vivid detail. Noises like we'd heard the night before, trying to sleep at the Hotel Villa Iguana: roosters crowing constantly, political loudspeakers blasting the night, but mostly, the music. The insufferably loud, booming, quaking, woofering music pumped into the atmosphere like mushroom clouds of methyl-ethyl-diesel exhaust: an in-your-face, conga-techno-rap explosion born from the hyper desire to make use of an earsplitting technology just because it's possible. Some may call it celebration, others may call it noise pollution, but it was definitely five hundred thousand watts of WHOMPF-WHOMPF-WHOMPFing island pop that some can tolerate better than others.

And once again, there it was, blasting the atmosphere. The beach was filled with hundreds of spring-break Westerners in Bermuda shorts and thong bikinis drinking Presidente Beer as they oohed in awe at the fish coming in. There'd been a week-long fishing tournament, and the local vendors were out in force, selling trinkets, hawking amber, mongering Hawaiian shirts made in Mexico. And contributing to all this confusion THUMP-THUMP-THUMPing in the afternoon heat, was a deafening

11. Butchered barracuda. Photo by Lea Graham.

HUMPA-HUMPA-HUMPA wall of sound shaking like a gazillion maracas from two pairs of ten-foot speakers strapped to a tractor trailer, all of them aimed directly at us.

The chaos again. It was in the air, it was full of bass, and there was nothing we could do but pull up on the sand, get out, and wade straight into it.

We made our way to the weighing station where technicolored mahi-mahi and gothically spiked wahoo were dangling like sides of beef. There was even a behemoth barracuda about five feet long and fifty pounds, which is about as big as they get this side of the Florida Keys.

And in this chaos, a cleaning frenzy was going on. Fishermen were chopping fish, filleting fish, and saving the roe as a sloppy slew of innards washed its way across the beach.

That's when I noticed that the locals weren't holding back on the barracuda. They were gutting them and slicing them and taking them home, even those over ten pounds—ciguatera be damned!

So I went back to our boat, picked out a seven-pounder, and Eduardo offered to clean it for me. "Sí," I said, and he broke out a knife, chopped it into an accordioned chain of steaks, then sent us on our way.

We took it straight to Mama Rosa, a jolly chef who ran a chicken shack across from our hotel. We'd eaten there the night before, and she told us she would cook any fish we caught. But now that I was standing there with a questionable fish in my grip, she was shaking her head with a tight-lipped frown. Lea, however, told her that it was small enough to not be infected, and she finally gave in.

"*Frita* o *criolla*?" was the question, so we went with the latter. And an hour later, now drinking cold beers, Mama Rosa brought it out on a platter. The head was flayed right down the middle in all its eyeball-glaring glory, and even the cheek meat was exposed as if to say, "Hey, dig on in!" Not only that, but there were baseball-sized hunks of sweet, white cuda meat swimming in a mild brown sauce. And on the side: yellow rice with pigeon peas, sweet plantains, salad, beans.

It was a culinary masterpiece! A work of cooking art! A true performance poetry piece leading to the next obvious phase of this investigation: I put a forkful in my mouth.

12. Creole barracuda. Photo by Mark Spitzer.

Hmmm. Not bad. The texture was flaky and firm, but something wasn't gelling. Something wasn't great. The sauce was fine, but nothing special. Whereas the meat was inviting, the payoff seemed anticlimactic. We couldn't figure it out.

I reckoned this was a fish that depended on its sauce. If the sauce was transcendental, then that could elevate the taste—but it just wasn't there. I mean, it was a good clean-tasting fish, and it wasn't fishy-tasting at all, so it should taste excellent.

Lea agreed. She said it was okay, but that's all it was. Just okay.

Thus my conclusion, which is pretty much what most sources say: it's edible, but nothing to write home about.

Nevertheless, I write this. About a fish. About a culture. About two people who go to the Caribbean, get engaged, and envision a twister. One that arises from the threat of chaos, but never quite strikes. And then, just as instantly as tornados are prone to form and drop from the sky, they can just fade away. As chaos often does—with an eerie silence following the breaking waves. The one saving grace of all this being: we didn't get poisoned or washed out to sea.

Chaos. It's part of this island's identity. It's a force that destroys but also creates. That's what I was working with. That's what I was reflecting on:

the fact that all that destructive power can sometimes serve to connect exceptions to the rule—if you're lucky, that is.

And I am. And I know it. Because if it wasn't for the violence of mass migrations clashing and smashing and scattering humans all over place, I never would've met this person, who I'm more than fortunate to have in my life. And here I am, and there she is, both of us beaten by the waves but together in the darkening dusk, surrounded by barracuda; rotating cyclically, psychically, cyclonically. As the roosters crow. As the music thumps. As the tide crushes on—all through the Dominican night.

4

Sportfishing Gar

An Old Dog's Failure Proves a Point

GAR ARE A PARADOX. WITH THEIR PREHISTORIC ALLIGATOR heads and their armor-plated serpentine bodies, they're often regarded as fierce and fangy monster fish. On the other hand, they're also seen as lowly and lazy and not worth fighting. But in writing two books on the species, and in traveling the world to catch them, one thing I've seen during my research is a radical change in their public perception. More exposure to their real issues on TV along with a serious boost in the science has definitely led to more understanding of this fish. And as a general respect for the subspecies increases, their reputation grows as a novelty to be caught on lures and flies.

For me, however, it's always been juglines, limblines, trotlines, and traditional rod and reel. I'd caught tropical and Florida gar on crankbaits, alligator and shortnose on cut bait, and spotteds and longnose on live bait. But since all my attempts at rope lures had fallen flat, I decided it was time to finally get a handle on this specialized approach and find out for myself if gar can really be called "sport fish."

The idea of a rope lure is pretty simple: you take a length of white nylon rope, tie a basic knot on one end, then clip it off at whatever length you want. You then use a lighter to melt a spot on the top of the knot where you insert the hook of a jig head. After that, you unravel the strands. You then pull that lure through the water, and because the lure resembles a swishing baitfish, gars go nuts and end up tangling their teeth in the fibers. Different cultures have been practicing variations of this method for millennia with impressive results.

Anyway, I figured I should get out on Lake Conway where I live in Arkansas, which is nine miles long and has fifty-two miles of shoreline, most of it harboring spotted, shortnose, and longnose gar. In fact, I caught the state record spotted in that lake on a chicken liver once, a seven-pounder I stupidly threw back. Since then, a state record twelve-pound, five-ounce spotted was shot out there with a bow and arrow.

So I got my tackle together—some primitive rope lures I'd made a few years before and two spinning rigs—then hit the far side of the lake. It was marshy with lots of lily pads, and it was overcast. Still, it was the last week of April, the time of year that gar start getting hooked on my trotline, so I knew they were active. But mostly, I just wanted to get a feel for casting these lures again.

Paddling across the bay in my canoe, I got to the windless side of the bay sheltered by cypress and tupelo trees. There was vegetation to cast along with occasional rises and ripples on the surface letting me know that fish were there. Standing in the middle like a paddleboarder, taking a stroke then taking a cast, I worked my way along the shore, cranking rope lures at a steady pace. I'd read that you should reel with a stop-go-stop-go rhythm, allowing the lure to sink before snapping it back onto its course, simulating a fish in distress. But at that point, I just wasn't ready for that.

I was switching back and forth between the rods. One was a medium-weight Ugly Stik with ten-pound monofilament and a standard-size reel. I had a steel leader on that attached to an eight-inch rope lure. The other rod was an eight-foot medium-action rod wound with ten-pound woven line. I had a shorter lure on that pole, maybe four inches long.

It didn't take long to get a feel for how to cast and for the speed necessary to keep the rope lure just under the surface where it could be seen. I also began to get a better sense for how these lures operate. They really do look like swimming fish, and when you twitch them a

13. Homemade rope fly (*bottom*) and eBay rope
lures (*top*). Photo by Mark Spitzer.

bit they resemble frogs pulling their legs into their bodies, then kicking
out to propel themselves forward.

I also found that half the time I brought in a rope lure it was tangled
up in itself. The problem was that sometimes when the lure went flying
through the air, the strands would wrap around the hook shaft between
the jig head and the top of the knot. After a while, those trailing fibers
knotted up and lost their free-flowingness. A comb, I thought, would've
been good to have had along because by the end of the afternoon those
lures looked like Cousin Itt from *The Addams Family.*

Later that day I got on eBay and found a number of rope lures. They
had better-designed heads, some of them just small weighted rings with
strands trailing directly behind, so there was less extra space to get tangled
in when being flung through the air. Others had built-in egg-shaped
weights at the top, and others had spinners attached. I ordered three
different varieties, and they showed up three days later.

I got out on the lake two more days that week, both times during dusk. In both cases, it hadn't been a very hot afternoon, which lowered my odds. The legendary gar man Jack Barnett who designed his own line of rope lures used to guide for longnose in Georgia, but only after noon when the sun was high in the sky. Following his example, I didn't see any reason to get up before dawn to fish for gar.

Chucking those lures and bringing them in, I was still trying to get a feel for the technique, and I was also searching for a garful spot. In the process, I saw the gar rise, most of them in the weeds. So I pulled those lures through the weeds using the fancy eBay lures on the pole strung with monofilament and my butt-ugly homemade lure on the pole with braided line. What I learned is that you can cast right into the alligator weed, and since there's no hook to catch on anything, you can slide them over lily pads and maneuver between water plants.

The fourth day was sunnier, and I got out in the afternoon with my buddy Goggle Eye. We launched at Caney Creek and motored down to the lake in my resurrected 1959 runabout with batwing fins, then drifted with the wind as it blew us upstream. There was tall grass on both sides, and it was warm enough that the water snakes were crossing the channel. I was standing and casting on the back bench which allowed me to see fish on the surface, but it just wasn't hot enough for the gar to want to catch some rays. I could also see my rope lures gliding through the water, so I began to experiment more with how to make them undulate. After a couple hours of experimental twitching, not catching anything, it just started coming naturally. That is, I got a way better feel for how to feel the rising, diving action.

Another thing I learned was that the best way to cast as far as possible—so as to get as much mileage out of a rope lure as you can—is to load it up with water right before you let it zing. This often left Goggle Eye with a splatter across his back as my rope lure sailed over his head, but he didn't seem to mind. I apologized a few times, but there was no way to avoid the curse. I tried to cast to the side, but the spray continued whipping him.

The fifth time out did the trick. It was eighty-something degrees, the sun was high in the sky, the wind was low, and Goggle Eye and I were in my flat-bottom boat, a twelve-footer with a two-horse two-stroke on the back. We'd left from my house and had motored a half-mile down the shore to a shallow part of the lake that was low on development. As usual, Goggle Eye was up front, this time using live crickets, whereas I was in back standing over the engine, feet planted against the gunwales. It was kind of precarious but no less tippy than standing up in a canoe.

There were plenty of swirls on the surface. We saw catfish coming up, shad plipping all around, and even a monster bowfin came over and took a glug of air just six feet from us. That bowfin must've weighed at least ten pounds, and it let us get an awesome visual of all its details down to its ganoid scales. And there were gar as well, rolling on the surface and slashing their tails. They were mostly on the edges of the weeds, so that's where I focused my rope lures and Goggle Eye put his bait.

My back was acting as a sail, the wind slowly blowing us along a bank of lily pads. Goggle Eye kept getting bites, which we figured were bluegills, but he was having trouble sealing the deal. After a few missed opportunities, we found out why. He was bringing a fish in, and it was darting around at right angles like a sunfish, but when he got it up to the surface we saw that it was a small gar shaking its head from side to side.

I dropped the net into the lake, but when Goggle Eye led it in, it suddenly leapt and spit out the hook. We saw it in the air: a beautiful mini-longnose.

Anyhow, we fished some more, and Goggle Eye kept missing them. He asked me if I'd like to use any of his crickets, but I declined, choosing to stick with this method if it took all summer.

In the meantime, I was finally starting to sense the proper flex and flux of the lure, even if I was losing faith. I was alternating rods, each of which had a different feel, and my back was beginning to ache from casting for hours, but I was now on a different plane. In fact, I was feeling graceful—or the lure was feeling graceful going through the water. It'd just come to the point where I could feel the right sway and play with my eyes closed.

That's when it hit, just like that. A definite fish was on, and there being only one fish in this system that could actually snag its teeth on a rope lure, it was obvious what it was. Then it came splashing in on the surface, a twenty-inch gar, all dark and spotty on the top and shiny white on the bottom, flipping and flapping all over the place.

"Get the net!" I shouted to Goggle Eye, and he got it in the water lickety-split. I pulled that thrashing gar right in, and as soon as it was in, it wolfed down half the mesh. I'm serious. That gar wound a vortex around its snout in such a death roll that there would be no plucking of strings from its teeth to free it. I had to break out a knife and cut it out, leaving two gaping holes in the net.

That's the kind of havoc gar are notorious for causing in boats, and my adrenaline was pumping from the quality of fight it had honored me with. That fish had fought as respectably as any northern pike, and not only that, it had given my medium-weight rod a workout. It was a healthy, strong, four-pound fish, and guess which lure it had gone for? It wasn't one of those specialized ones I'd ordered off eBay. Nope, it was my dirty, dingy, hillbilly model full of twigs and burrs and who knows what. It basically looked like a snarly old dreadlock dredged up from a river bottom—but man, it had done its job and done it well!

After that, there was no way I could resist taking sportfishing for gar to the next level: fly fishing—which I'd been avoiding for years. Why? Because this approach was as foreign to me as walking on the moon. I'd tried it before with nothing but frustration as the end result, but now it was time to try again. So I blew the dust off my fly rod and hit the lake.

It didn't take long to recall why I was a rookie with this type of angling. It had been years since a crotchety old guy from the fly shop had given me a lesson. He kept barking at me that I was doing it all wrong, so I went rogue and developed my own barbaric technique, which is why I kept tangling my fly in the line. Nevertheless, I regained a feel for how to get a fly fifteen to twenty feet from the boat, and I knew that if the sun was high and I saw a gar within range I could plop a fly in front of it and start stripping in line.

But the sun wasn't high in the sky. In fact, it was practically nonexistent, which made it less likely that a gar would give a wang dang doodle

14. Four-pound spotted gar on rope lure. Photo by Scotty Lewis.

if it even saw my fly. Gar, of course, are more active when the weather is warm, and it was a chilly spring.

Still, I went out a few times, and I watched a few videos in which anglers just as lousy at fly casting as me managed to land some gar. I was heartened by the idea that if those guys could do it, so could I.

I also knew that I had to get better faster because my house was up for sale. It looked like I had a buyer, and I would be moving soon, which would eat into my gar-flying time. So I gave ol' Bill Wilmert a call. He's a fishing guide up in Heber Springs who'd written a book called *Fly Fishing on the Red*. Bill and his wife Donna have sixteen International Game Fish Association (IGFA) records between them for catching different types of gar on different weight lines.

"Come on up," Bill said, "and we'll work on your cast."

So I went on up, and he showed me the appropriate grip and how to hold my elbow and how to make a loop unfurl in the air, then accelerate and plop in the right spot. We were whizzing that fly across the parking lot where a Styrofoam cup played the part of a lollygagging gar just nosing along on the surface. Bill had promised to show me some tricks which would double the distance I could cast, and I almost met that mark.

But I hadn't gone up there just for that. First of all, I'd gone there to meet Bill, and secondly, there were other areas I knew he could assist me with. As Bill had told me, gar were his favorite fish, and since he was a storehouse of information on how to fly fish for gar, and since he had a solid history of getting them, I knew he could help me with gear as well, and what type of line to use, and advice on how to set the hook. Plus, I was just plain ignorant when it came to fly-line leaders and tying knots.

Fortunately, Bill was one hell of a teacher. This wasn't because he was a professional guide who knew how to connect people with fish; it was more because of his user-friendly demeanor. The lesson Bill gave was essentially a conversation. He asked me questions about what I was doing, which made me realize what I needed to adjust. He also had a great sense of humor, and he said some things that I couldn't help agreeing with.

Like how the spotteds are his favorite kind of gar because they're the most beautiful, a statement I could get on board with. I never get tired of those obsidian leopard spots adding contrast to the snaky silver of a gar.

The subject of color came up again when Bill brought up the concept of sport fish:

"I talk to all these guys who are into bass," he told me, "and I say you call a two-pound plain brown fish like that a sport fish?" Then holding his arms four feet apart, he said, "This is what I call a sport fish! Something with teeth an inch long that can bite the living crap out of you!"

We also had a conversation about guys who catch gars and immediately break off their beaks, which I mentioned was happening a lot less these days since that older generation of gar-hating intolerants was dying out along with their bias. Or, at least, that was my hope in an age in which a new slew of fishing show hosts was passing on a respect for the environment. When angling personalities on TV and the internet catch and release fish and talk about ecology and the roles that maligned fish play in maintaining balance, that information goes straight to the core of the couch-potato consciousness, which is evolving a more informed outlook toward the idea of conservation. Or maybe that's just my hope again.

Anyway, hopping in my Jeep with a new supply of googly-eyed grasshopper flies and albino wooly buggers, I shot back to Lake Conway more fortified in gar-fly-fishing knowledge than I'd ever been. I'd gotten the gar-fly dope directly from the gar-fly master, who'd been generous enough to gift out his experience for a reason as simple as sharing what you love with others so that they can gain what you've got. Basically, he was passing on a skillset for hooking a fish that's common in this country yet hardly ever recognized as a worthy opponent to do battle with.

But as Bill told me before I left, "You still need two more casting lessons."

Then months went by as I cast and cast.

I started with one of the grasshopper flies, the voice of Bill in my head telling me to keep my wrist straight. But since the real Bill wasn't there coaching me, I soon slipped back to my caveman ways, casting mainly by feel. It was a mixture of instincts informed by lessons, and I wasn't really doing that badly. I could get it out there twenty, maybe thirty feet from the flat-bottom boat, and that's all I needed. Or so I figured.

It was a windy day. Too windy and cloudy out. The wind kept slapping my fly around and putting up resistance. But since these are conditions you have to deal with in the field, I was glad for the practice.

On the way home, though, I hit a log and busted the hub that holds the propeller to the shaft. So now that this mode of floatation was toast, at least temporarily, I made some changes in my approach.

The first was going back to the canoe. I went out on a day with a lot less wind, exploring the weedlines. I was acquiring more of a feel for casting flies, but the thing was, I kept ignoring Bill's advice. What felt natural just felt workable, so my backhand was going out to four o'clock, then coming down at eight, not hitting the appropriate two and ten. By the time I started getting that fly past thirty feet, I was getting pretty good at getting it to go where I wanted it to go.

The third time out I switched to a white wooly bugger and got more used to making it undulate. Stripping it in, I experimented with different lengths and different speeds, and I also tried a new casting method. Casting out as far as I could, I'd let it land, let out some line, then backcast that rather than trying to let out line in the air. That way I could snap it up from the water in front of me, then let it land behind me without having to keep an eye on what happens in the sky. I'd do that a few times, and then it would be almost forty feet out.

But I wasn't catching anything. That is, until an accidental fish suddenly erupted when a backcast landed in the lake. I missed that mystery fish, but it left me with an increased heart rate banging in my chest. Something had happened, which meant I was on the right track.

The next time out, skootching around in the lily pads, the midday sun beating down, I came to regret my experimental belligerence. By plopping that fly into the water in front of me and behind me every time I took a cast, I hooked a lily pad stem. When I cast forward, the pole broke. Or, I should say, that fly rod snapped with a shattering sound that sounded exactly like "HOLY CRAP! THERE GOES 180 BUCKS!" I instantly lost three inches of rod, as well as some flexibility and overall casting range, but I got the busted chunk out and managed to fit the pieces back together.

Then a gar actually struck. I saw it just a few yards from the boat, white and twisting in the water, and its flash was more than a flash of hope. It was a flash that affirmed that the more I spun the gar roulette wheel, the more likely it would land on my number. But I didn't tighten up in time. That gar got off and slashed away.

As the summer continued, I sold my house and upgraded to the other side of the lake. A yard sale happened, moving took place, and I had to contend with fixing stuff and buying stuff and all that junk you have to do, which cut into my fishing time.

Then, when June rolled around, Lea and I got married in the foothills of the Catskills where I was able to practice my tactics for a month in a new wild place. Walking upstream in those crystal-clear creeks, I fished for bluegills and smallmouth bass. Seeing those fish plain as day just brought back something from my youth. It was an excitement I hadn't known since I was a kid nabbing minnows with my onion-sack net. Now, however, my tool was a fly rod, because I was practicing for gar. And with every beautiful rock bass I caught via my guerilla ways, and with every fat carp and channel cat I glimpsed, the more of a feel I got for putting that fly exactly where I wanted it. Almost all my coaching had gone down the drain, but hell, I was getting 'em!

To the point that I put my masterplan into action by hiring gar guru Drew Price, who might just be the world's most well-known fly-fishing gar guide. We made arrangements to meet on the Vermont side of Lake Champlain. When I arrived, the sun was high and the water was clear. Ospreys were soaring everywhere, and I figured this chapter would soon be over.

Wrong-O!

We stepped into his modified canoe: a fifteen-foot flat-back with a tunnel hull. It was equipped with pontoons on both sides to add stability, and as we paddled out to his secret cove, we exchanged stories of being on *River Monsters*, me on the "Alligator Gar" episode and him on "Vampires of the Deep."[1] In investigating landlocked sea lampreys with a thirst for blood on Lake Champlain, Drew had led the world's foremost "freshwater detective" to bowfin and gar. In fact, there was a scene shot between Jeremy Wade's legs of him lifting a bowfin with a fish gripper, which I had laughed at because his ass was so prominent in the shot. But as it turned out, that was Drew's rear end. "Ha!" I had joked. "You're Jeremy's butt double!"

That's when we saw our first longy of the day, or *chaousarou* as the Iroquois used to call them. In my first gar book, I'd studied this lake for the monster myth of "Champ" and had made the claim that since the French explorer Samuel de Champlain had noted two rows of teeth on the chaousarou, this was evidence that alligator gar had ranged as far north as the Canadian border four hundred years ago.[2] Then, in my second gar book, I'd refuted a biologist who had publicly rejected that claim.[3] But now . . . now I was reconsidering my claim about the northernmost range of alligator gar. No game-changing evidence of gator gar this far north had ever been offered, and longnose had always been up here, so that's probably what Champlain had seen. The splashing of their spawning is most likely what various witnesses described as Nessie's North American cousin, the fabled crypto-plesiosaur stalking this legendary loch.

But back to that fat chaousarou skimming along on the sandy flats. It was a big thick forty-incher, which I instantly thought was an alligator gar because it was so huge. It was in a foot and a half of water, and Drew told me to go for it.

I took his nine-foot, nine-weight Orvis rod strung up with specialized line (plus a nine-foot tippet made from twenty-five-, eighteen-, and thirty-pound fluorocarbon), and I cast one of his custom-made flies right in front of it. Though it was a slovenly cast, I hit my mark. But that gar, it was on to us, and it wasn't gonna fall for none of our shenanigans.

I should describe that fly, which is one of the reasons I chose to fish with Drew. Since I was trying to catch a gar with a fly, and since the

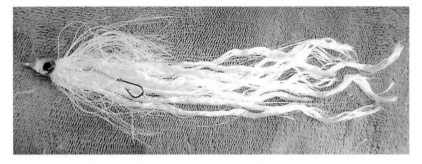

15. Green-and-white gar fly by Drew Price, six
inches long. Photo by Mark Spitzer.

traditional flies I'd tried hadn't worked, I was intrigued by his rope-lure
flies as a compromise. Made primarily from white nylon rope, they have
squid-eye jig heads, and they're trimmed with a bit of sparkle in the
strands. But they also have a #6 hook hanging in there due to the local
fishing laws which require hooks.

Essentially, I was fudging a bit with my mission to hook a gar on a
conventional fly, but what kept me honest was the fly rod. I was still on
unfamiliar turf trying to figure out the casting and stripping in, I wasn't
taking the easy way out, and I knew these flies would up my odds of
connecting with a gar, so that's what I was doing now.

More importantly, I'd revealed my shoddy technique to Drew, who
insisted on dropping anchor to give me an emergency casting lesson.
Ugh, I thought, resisting at first, since prior lessons had sent me packing
with the attitude that I'd learn how to do it on my own. It's always hard
to teach an old dog to want to learn new tricks, but what the heck? I
gave in and practiced what he preached—which, again, was two and ten
o'clock. And straighten that wrist. And strip it in like this. And place
your thumb up higher. Etcetera.

Anyway, we got back on the hunt, Drew standing in back, poling us
through the weeds, me casting up front. The ospreys were spiraling
above, and one even dove twenty yards off the bow, smacking the water
and grabbing a fish. It was the closest I'd ever been to an osprey dive,
but our eyes were mostly pegged on the weeds.

There were carp abounding and other fish visible in the milfoil and water chestnut and other invasives vying for space among the cattails and lily pads. From his vantage point in back, Drew was scanning the cove for activity, and from my spot on the bow, I could see pretty much everything within a thirty-foot diameter. Then I saw one, just chilling in a hole in the weeds. It was a three-foot tubular gar pointing away from me.

It took two crappy casts, but I got Drew's fly in front of it, and just like that it snapped. And just like that I flinched, yanking the fly right out of its mouth. My intention had been to start tugging that longy through the weeds, but in setting the hook, the most natural of reactions an angler can have, I lost that beautiful fish.

Drew razzed me for that in a consoling way, and we got back to business. Within an hour, we saw two more gar, both of them the same size as the one I'd missed. They were in the zone that I could see in front of me, which Drew couldn't see because of me. So both times I spotted them, we were basically on top of them. Consequently, they saw us and sashayed off.

We cruised around all afternoon, Drew shoving through the weedy muck, me scanning as far as I could and blind-casting to improve my technique. But that was it for gar. A weird eastern wind began rippling the surface and making it difficult to spot fish, so I ended up taking home something else that was a far cry from a chaousarou. Mainly this:

The fish mission I'd picked—to catch a gar with a fly—was one of the most difficult investigations I had ever undertaken. Like muskie hunting—which had taken me an entire summer, five guides and thousands of dollars—this type of fishing was not for amateurs.

But the main thing I got, which Drew dubbed my "ah-ha moment," came in the form of a twist tie from Home Depot. It got to the point, I think, that he just couldn't stand me casting limp-wristedly in the same way that French people can't stand to hear me butcher their language. He grabbed a piece of plastic-coated wire and wrapped it around my rod-hand wrist and the rod. Then suddenly I had a splint, and it kept me from bending my wrist. The result being an instantaneous improvement with two and ten o'clock.

"Now put a bit more snap into your backhand," he advised, and I decided not to be a wimp. I put some more snap into it, and then we worked on my release. He told me to let it go at the bottom of the arc, then lower the rod after that. I did that, and it shot across the lake like a bullet. It cleared forty feet, and Drew cheered.

That was definitely one of the two casting lessons Bill Wilmert told me I needed, so I'm still in need of another. In the meantime, I know I have a lot to learn, especially in comparison to the true poets of the craft I've been studying. Seeing the grace of experienced fly anglers unravel before my eyes gives me something to aspire to. Thus, with sincere respect for the patience and precision it takes to wield a fly rod properly, I bow down to an art I used to rail against like an adolescent punk whose complaints about the bourgeoisie are now as transparent as the tippet on the end of my line.

That's where I wish this "teachable moment" actually ended, with the knowledge that even though I couldn't land the fish I'm supposed to know best, the possibility remains that we can transcend the hurdles that make our lives interesting and sometimes even worth living. Because gar aren't just trash fish or lethargic fish we think we know: they're an extremely challenging sport fish that can lead to addiction. So you gotta watch out, because there's a price we all pay for the contracts we make with ourselves. And the fact that I'm still out there casting like a maniac, that's actually evidence of the highly specialized skill it takes to catch a gar on the fly.

But like I said, that's the way I wish this fish tale would've ended; but it didn't. In all honesty, I found this mania something that I had to put down because of the time it was taking away from other fish. And since this wasn't something that I had to get done or the whole world would explode, I decided to put this pursuit on hold.

Because ultimately, fly fishing for gar was something I could always return to. And at that moment, driving back through upstate New York with the radio reminding me of all that was at stake in the world, I knew

I had to make my overall monster-fish mission less of a how-to narrative and more of something else. And since I could tell in my gut that I was closing in on whatever I was fishing for, I was glad to take a break on gar.

In other words, there were vital new oceans to explore, and in order to seriously "be good for something" as Thoreau advised, I knew I had to step even further outside my comfort zone.[4] So I set my sights on even stranger monster fish and put the hammer down.

5

Monster-Fishing Shark Off Montauk

Reframing the Narratives of Fisheries and Ourselves

WHEN I SET OFF FOR MONTAUK ON THE EASTERNMOST TIP of Long Island to check out the highly popular sport of shark hunting, I had a few questions about the apex predators I was going after. First, what's the deal? I mean, what's the attraction, how did it come about, and why does it endure? Then secondly, where do you put a shark in a boat when there's only an eight-by-six-foot area to move around in on the stern, and it's filled with coolers and buckets and fishing gear? Plus, there's this built-in contraption right in the middle of the deck with cables and clips all over it that's called a "fishing post," which is where you strap a pole to crank in a big fish. And thirdly, what happens to the thousands of sharks caught annually on rod and reel, not just in New York state, but all over the world? Do sharks die in the process? Can you cook 'em? Or is it mostly catch and release?

Whatever the case, I knew this investigation would be important. Since sharks are top predators, and since food chains hinge on what's at the tops and bottoms of their complex interconnecting networks, the health and security of these extremes affect environmental balance worldwide. Through years of research on gar, for example, I'd learned that the conservation statuses of alligator gar influence all populations of rough fish and catfish and crayfish in a system, so if you allow for a species at the top of a chain to be extirpated, then you can expect organisms in the middle to become anemic.

Meanwhile, we're seeing an average of 100 million sharks disappearing every year. That's one-third the population of the United States, a number that's mind-boggling. Of course, some of those sharks are harvested for food, like in Australia where they're used for fish and chips, or in Japan and India where their meat is also a traditional staple. Still, Asian countries are taking a big chomp out of this market due to the popularity of shark fin soup, which is rumored to have medicinal qualities, particularly as an aphrodisiac. Mostly, though, shark fin soup is a symbol of wealth and prestige, particularly in China. People spend up to $400 per bowl to show off how cool they are by slurping down a tasteless broth. That's why we have the practice of "shark finning," meaning catching sharks and chopping off their dorsal fins, then throwing the fish back to die. Also, the historical belief that sharks are full of supernutrients is total bull. They're actually full of mercury from eating fish on a planet fueled by coal-burning power plants.

The upshot being: whether or not recreational shark hunting is a sport or a tourist industry or both, or just a drop in the bucket compared to commercial shark fishing (black market and legit), there are more than five hundred species in the world. According to Oceana, "Scientists estimate that fishing has reduced large predatory fish populations worldwide by 90 percent over the past 50 to 100 years. Sharks now represent the largest group of threatened marine species."[1] In fact, according to the IUCN, "A quarter of the world's sharks and rays are threatened with extinction," a figure that doubles depending on location and species.[2]

I met Captain John Krol on his boat dubbed *Let's Go Fishin*. It was a foggy July morning when we motored out of the Star Island Yacht Club, which was more of a mooring than a status symbol for this salt-of-the-earth, old-school shark guide who'd been chartering such trips since 1980. That was almost forty years ago, which I figured was close to half his life. With his orange suspendered rubber pants and congenial

16. Bizarre photo of a shark-finning wedding.
Courtesy of Saatchi & Saatchi, Singapore.

attitude, Captain Krol was a trim and weathered veteran of the region with the experience necessary to connect me with what I'd come to get.

He also had the gear: mostly giant baitcasting reels on heavy-duty megarods sporting pop-bottle-sized Styro-floats. The poles were strung with 100-pound monofilament, and there were two-ounce egg weights right beneath the floats with rubber bands attached to them for a purpose I'll explain later. Each rig also had a shock leader (or "dog leash"), and a 175-pound wire leader (or "piano string") attached to an extralarge, no-thrills, big-game J-hook. It was the kind of equipment that foreshadowed monster fish, and I was pumped to be chugging past the jetty. We then shot out to sea, cutting through fog so thick we could hardly see thirty yards in any direction.

Having just come back from a honeymoon in Borneo, I had a major case of jet lag. The night before, I just couldn't sleep and only nodded off for an hour. It was one of those nights where I was laying there counting hundreds of Mississippis while wondering what the day would bring. So now I was wondering if I'd pass out on the boat or be too fatigued to reel in a shark. Or like some similarly sleepless nights before going after muskellunge and sturgeon, would the excitement of the hunt keep me awake?

Hell if I knew. What I did know was that the boat was rising and diving across the swells, and I had one day to make it happen. Because if I didn't connect with a shark, any shark, that would be more than a thousand dollars down the drain. But worse than that, it would be a missed opportunity to get answers to my shark-hunting questions, which I suspected pertained to a larger context.

It took over an hour to get to the spot, which I can only describe as out in the middle of nowhere. The fog had burned off, the sun was rising higher, and the sea had calmed. Captain Krol turned the boat so that the breeze was broadsiding it, then cut the motor and dropped in the thawing "bunker chum," which was blood, viscera, and chunks of oily menhaden meat. It was in a five-gallon bucket with strainer holes drilled in it, and it was tied to the rail.

The chum slick spread out instantly, small chunks filtering out. This immediately attracted some shearwaters and gulls. These guys, maybe five at the most, then followed us for the rest of the day, nabbing scraps.

The chum, however, also attracted another creature. I saw its dark dorsal fin breach amidst the birds and recognized it right off the bat. It was a porpoise porpoising. In fact, it was three porpoises porpoising. Side by side, they rose and dove, which Captain Krol said was a good sign. It meant that there were fish in these waters, so sharks would come around.

"The water here is a nice and clean seventy degrees," the captain told me, letting out line on a rod. He set it about forty yards away from the boat, dangling a Boston mackerel twenty feet beneath the surface. According to the depth finder, it was 177 feet deep.

Captain Krol then let out the line on another rod. This one had a bunker on it, and he set that float about twenty feet from the rail.

Since the drift fishing had begun, I decided to pump my guide for information. "So," I asked, "how has this fishery changed since the eighties?"

"I don't care where you are," he replied, "fishing's down everywhere. There's so much fishing pressure . . . commercial as well as recreational."

He then told me about the drop in striped bass through the decades, and the drop in sharks as well. He'd never seen many great whites, but he'd caught plenty of makos and threshers and blues. The browns were rarer, but every year, whatever the species, there were always less than the year before.

The time was right to ask my question about the popularity of shark hunting, and how this phenomenon got its start. Captain Krol explained that it used to be all about tuna out here, but when the tuna thinned due to the mushrooming markets, something else had to take its place. Shark then became the thing. There were plenty around, they were exciting to fight, they were pretty much all trophy size, and the sport grew with the tourism.

"Before that," Captain Krol added, "there was only one shark hunter in these waters . . . Frank Mundus. After trying to kill everything in the ocean, he became a conservationist . . . then tried to save everything in it."

Ah, Frank Mundus. I'd been hoping to touch on this subject, which is basically unavoidable in Montauk. He's in the gift shops, on t-shirts and caps and coffee mugs. He's definitely in the culture and consciousness of these shores. But mostly, he's in the movies. Mundus was the model for the Ahabesque Quint character in *Jaws*, which changed the way the world thinks about sharks. Not only did that sensational Hollywood film inspire an entire subgenre of B-horror flicks for generations to come, it also created a climate of fear that is in no way proportional to the real amount of shark attacks that happen on an annual basis. Essentially, throughout the world, there have only been two thousand verified shark attacks in two thousand years—most of them from white, tiger, and bull sharks.

My focus, though, wasn't concerned with the mythologies and hype of the shark's place in pop culture or facts concerning shark biology, which others have covered way better than I could ever hope to repeat. My focus was environmental, which is why "Monster Man" Frank Mundus, who inspired the concept of "monster fishing," was of interest to me.

With his hoop earring and shark-tooth necklace, and his two big toenails painted green and red (one for starboard, the other for port), he was a colorful character, as well as the subject of a few documentaries and TV shows. He used to kill 4,500-pound great whites with harpoons, and he was famous for catching a 3,427-pounder on a fishing pole despite having a crippled left arm. The latter lunker is sometimes considered the world record for rod and reel, but other times it's debated. That shark had been feeding on a dead whale when Mundus hooked it, and there's a controversy about whether its capture was legal.

What intrigued me most was Mundus's come-to-Jesus moment, or whatever it was that made him change the massacring ways he used to be renowned for, shooting and spearing and blowing sharks up with hand grenades. From the research I've done, I can't say what triggered that change, but I can note a couple things he did to change his image. He promoted circle hooks as a way of catching sharks in their jaws rather than in their guts to help increase their chances of survival after letting them go. And according to the *New York Times*, he "helped start a shark-tagging program and voiced support for catch-and-release fishing."[3]

Mundus' last interview from 2013 includes a moment of disturbing speculation. When asked where he believes American fisheries will be in fifty years, he replied, "They won't have any fish in the ocean. They're taking all the fish out. When you have a fish bowl, and you take all the fish out of the fish bowl . . . you don't have any more fish."[4]

Thus, a new question arises: is removing 100 million sharks per year the equivalent of taking all the fish out of a fish bowl?

At first this sounds like a ridiculous question, but since our actions have consequences, it's not unreasonable to consider—especially if we start seeing a radical change in a chain we all depend on. After all, chains are subject to chain reactions, so all it takes is one compromised link, and everything goes straight to hell.

"This is the boring part," Captain Krol said an hour later. We'd been watching the birds and the floats with no action whatsoever, and I knew his tone well. It's what fishing guides say when they take out clients with high expectations, and the bite just isn't on. But having been in this position many times before, I was aware of the gamble it always is. You either get action or you don't, and the weather and other factors play a role in what your odds really are.

"I prefer to look at it as 'relaxing,'" I replied, shooting to reframe the situation. I see plenty of guides with their reputations on the line trying to drum up fish, and I always feel their anxiousness when things get difficult.

So we waited and waited all morning long as Jesus birds came fluttering by. They were these little black and white suckers that landed on the water and skittered on the surface, seemingly walking on the waves.

Still, I kept my eyes pegged on those floats, even though the stretch of the horizon left more to the imagination. Since I'd been waiting months to do this research, I wasn't about to let those floats out of my sight. The moment something happened, I was prepared to react.

My lack of sleep, however, was beginning to catch up with me. Luckily, I ate a sandwich around eleven, and that gave me some staying power.

We drifted for miles, and the sun got hotter. The captain had thawed out another chum bucket, and he was spooning it over the rail every five minutes. We were each working equally as hard, even if some might see it as us just sitting there not saying nothing.

But sometimes we talked. Captain Krol told me about how he got pulled over for having a headlight out and the process he had to go through to avoid a ticket, and I talked about similarities in shark and gar fishing. With both of these creatures, the idea is that when they work, you don't. And when they don't work, you should. Meaning using the drag to tire them out and reeling in when you lower the rod. Plus letting them run, then waiting for them to slow or stop before setting the hook.

But by two in the afternoon, after staring at those floats for hours with nothing appearing except two vivid hallucinations of shadows I thought were fish backs rising, it got too hard to stay awake. The sun was now pretty intense. My skin was burning and the shade of the cabin was calling to me. I was teetering there, drifting off, in danger of falling overboard. So after what seemed like an entire shark week of struggling to stay awake, I swallowed my pride, went inside, stretched out, blacked out, and slept hard for ten minutes straight.

That's all I needed to snap back. And when I did, I felt strangely rejuvenated. But emerging from the cabin, I knew that we'd already spent eight hours on the water, and my time was up. We still had an hour and a half of motoring back, and I was keeping my guide overtime. Basically, we were both embarrassed: him for not producing a shark, and me for keeping him on the water when he had things to do.

"Okay then," I muttered, "let's pack it up."

Then suddenly a fin! Just like in the movies! It was right beneath the closest float, only twenty feet from the boat. Another hallucination, I figured. But after I blinked it was still there, along with perforated gill slits and two elegant pectoral fins. It was slowly moving toward the boat.

"Shark," I whispered, and pointed it out.

It was heading right toward the chum bucket, clearly interested in the stench. Like a blue catfish, it had a silky shine to it. There were a couple skinny, zebra-striped fish swimming alongside it, and then it was under the boat.

Captain Krol pulled the bait over to the boat, which is what I was hoping he'd do. The shark emerged below the stern, then circled back toward the bucket. It didn't seem extremely excited, but I definitely was as it passed by again. It was heading toward the waterlogged bunker that had been hanging there all day.

Then the float began to move. Not back and forth or erratically, but in little shivery micromotions because the shark was going down. Then it took the float completely down, causing the rubber band to snap. The float shot up, signaling that the shark was making a run, even if it was at a casual gait. It was towing the float out to sea as the captain removed the pole from its holder and handed it to me. I accepted the rig and positioned my thumb right above the sluggishly unspooling line.

"Are you ready?" he asked, and I confirmed. When the fish slowed, he flipped the lever into the strike zone and gave me the nod.

Hauling back, I felt the mass, I felt the meat. The rod began to bow. It wasn't dramatic, but it was on. Like a log.

Then it cut in the other direction, heading toward the other float. I pointed this out as we locked my pole into the fishing post, and the captain grabbed the other reel. The lines got crossed, but it was no biggie. As I cranked down, bringing the fish in, he passed his pole under mine. It took a few tries, and it also took some backtracking, but he managed to get the mess untangled.

Two minutes later, the shark was right under us. It was just swishing in place next to the boat.

"He's very cooperative," Captain Krol stated, almost apologetically.

We could see it and it could see us, but it wasn't afraid. Maybe it had been in this position before and knew it would soon be freed. Or maybe it was just a big, old, lazy lug.

I snapped a few pictures, and he brought out the snips. In another couple minutes, it would all be over, so I put in a special request.

"Can we let it out for another run?"

"Sure."

So we let the shark out for another run, and it shot off with a bit more spunk. I let it go about thirty yards, then started cranking down again. And again, it came in.

This time, when I got it up the boat, it resisted. Thrashing its tail, it disrupted the surface, and when I lifted its head out of the water, it shook and splashed around.

The captain grabbed the leader, and the fish twisted, starting to get pissed. We were messing with it, and it was not amused.

Now it was time to find out the answer to my question about what happens next. Would we rope its tail and bring it into the boat or would we release it in the water?

"If it was a mako or a thresher, we could bring it back," Captain Krol told me, which I was strangely pulled to do for the novelty of cooking it and knowing it better. Which felt weird: to know that I'm for catch and release, and that this species is vulnerable, yet there I was wanting to keep a beautiful fish that Captain Krol claimed was too dangerous to have slapping around in the boat.

At least this answered my question about where you'd put a shark in this space. If it was under six feet, Captain Krol said there was room in the aft end to take it back. If it was bigger than that, and if the client insisted on keeping it, he would tow it back.

"How big do you suppose it is?" I changed the subject.

"Seven and a half feet . . . maybe 170 pounds. Two hundred at the most."

So there I had it, the second largest fish I'd ever caught, at least a foot longer than me and probably more in weight.

"You ready to let it go?" he asked.

"Yep," I replied, and he cut the wire as close to the teeth as he could get.

It was anticlimactic watching that shark swoosh away, and at first I was bummed to not get the money shot. But as I sat there buzzing hard, rewinding and replaying the details in my head, I was glad I'd asked for that second run, and I was glad to have played it a second time and to have experienced more vigor on its part. But more than that, it was simply amazing to have those images in my brain: the electric blues of the water and sky and shark combined; the adrenal blasts that accompanied those long, graceful, winglike fins; the bright white of its belly; and the payoff in the end.

And the more I kept revisiting what I'd actually caught, the more and more glad I was. I mean, so what if I never touched it? Or got the cliché trophy shot? I had accomplished what I set out to do, my questions had been answered, and I knew it was juvenile to desire evidence to prove what I caught when I had these visions in my head. I also knew that according to IGFA rules, the fact that someone on board had touched

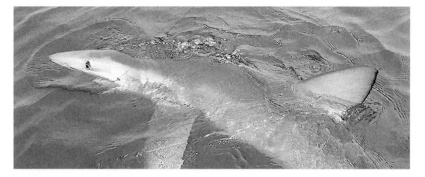

1 7. Blue shark. Photo by Mark Spitzer.

the leader meant I caught it. But ultimately, what mattered most was that the process had been humane.

First, the hook wasn't stainless steel. It was a plain old metal hook and would corrode away quickly. And secondly, we saved that fish a lot of stress. Sure, I'd provoked it a bit, and it had protested, but by leaving it in the water along with its dignity, we'd taken the higher road. Not only that, we'd foregone slopping blood all over the deck, and nobody got chomped. Its internal organs had not been abused by taking it out of the zero-gravity environment it was accustomed to, and the only elevated heartrate around was my own—to have been privileged enough to have met it.

This was another instance of reframing. In the same way I had reframed the concept of "boring" as "relaxing" (when "frustrating" might've been a more appropriate word), I was reframing my expectations according to what sharks actually need. They don't need posers manhandling them for photos taken at their expense, and we don't need to grandstand or risk injuries. It should be enough to be satisfied with the fact that we can encounter incredible fish that can school us on their mysteries.

But, I also noticed, there was another reframing in the works. I was flashing back to what Captain Krol had said about fish going down everywhere, and I wasn't completely convinced of the overall decline. Sure, world fisheries aren't what they used to be in comparison to the nineteenth century when 150-pound catfish weren't uncommon across the continent and white sturgeon grew twenty feet long and the cod fishery of the Grand Banks hadn't yet collapsed due to overharvesting. Still, we are making progress in reclaiming some of our overfished niches. We're reestablishing alligator gar, for instance, not just in the southern states but in more northern places throughout their native range. The Illinois Department of Natural Resources Division of Fisheries released 1,600 juvenile gator gar in 2017 as part of their Alligator Gar Reintroduction Program.[5] Also, we may not have as many stripers in the ocean as there used to be, but now that they're being stocked in force from coast to coast, they're more abundant in fresh water (e.g., the Georgia Department of Natural Resources adding 4.7 million stripers into the upper Coosa River between 1973 and 1992).[6]

In the meantime, at least in the United States, we're taking aggressive measures to protect shark fisheries. Off Montauk, there's a one-shark-per-day harvesting law for recreational anglers with a minimum length of fifty-four inches for permissible species. The National Oceanic and Atmospheric Administration, in partnership with the U.S. Department of Commerce, has established management plans and objectives. Also, Congress passed the Shark Finning Prohibition Act of 2000 to limit the amount of damage to sharks. There are loopholes, of course, and it's often two steps forward and one step back when we strive to protect species that other countries still eliminate willy-nilly, but for the reframing I need to do in order to stave off despair, I've got to reject the totalizing statement that our fish are going down everywhere. Because if I decide to see things that way, and if we all decide to see things that way, then there's no hope, so why even try?

That's why I did a completely uncharacteristic thing. I went to the cooler, and even though I knew a beer would wipe me out, I got myself an ice-cold IPA in the middle of the day. Then popping the top, I raised it to the sky—not in a toast to anything, but in general celebration of what we've got. Because what we've got is literally beyond awesome. And if we can let what we've got work its magic, that's enough to keep us *in awe* for a lifetime.

Just as quickly as I caught that shark, the fog rolled in and the wind came up. It got choppy, so we put the pedal to the metal, cruising through the ghostly gray. A gray so ghostly, in fact, that a fishing trawler emerged like an apparition. It had outrigger booms extending from both sides to drag giant nets which snag creatures that end up as collateral damage. Like dolphins, which are frequently pictured as the poster children for the price we pay for tuna fish. But beyond the tons of bycatch which get snuffed by commercial trawlers, there's the reality that when bottom trawling takes place marine environments get destroyed. Shellfish grounds are sacrificed. Microorganisms take a hit. All sorts of life gets smeared in the process.

But damn, that boat was dramatic! It looked like a haunted thing, and it burned its image into my brainpan in the same way the fish markets in Borneo did a week before. I'd seen the same tuna there that we have here being sold in sizes so scurvy you know it's a crime. One reason we're now running short on twelve-foot bluefins is because much more desperate countries with a lot less regulation and enforcement continue to allow for mass commercial molestation. It takes eight to twelve years for those tuna to reproduce, but we're not letting them get that old. In countless places all over the world, fish are being taken out of the equation before they even reach spawning size. Take bluefin tuna, for instance, whose populations, according to the *Guardian*, have "plummeted by 96% from unfished levels during nearly a century of overfishing."[7]

This is a travesty, and it's happening at a time when global marine populations have been gutted in comparison to decades before. As noted in the *Borneo Post*, for example, "over-fishing, pollution and climate change . . . between 1970 and 2010" have reduced the entire *Scombridae* fish family (which includes tuna, mackerel, and bonito) by 74 percent.[8] And as Marco Lambertini, head of the World Wildlife Fund (WWF),

18. Ghost trawler. Photo by Mark Spitzer.

states, "In the space of a single generation, human activity has severely damaged the ocean by catching fish faster than they can reproduce while also destroying their nurseries."[9]

In Malaysian waters, the widespread practice of taking immature fish out of the system was most visible to me with the yellowfin tuna at the Central Market in Kota Kinabalu. As you can see in the photo below, the sixteen-inch fish in the foreground and the foot-long fish behind it will never add their genetic stock to the wild populations swimming in the South China Sea. This species typically reach sexual maturity between twenty-one and twenty-six inches, but like fisheries all over the planet suffering from overfishing, especially in developing countries, the consequences are crystal clear: if you take immature fish out of a fishbowl, then they can't reproduce anywhere. So when you have 100 million sharks being removed from the system every year, along with the unquantifiable genocide of millions of tuna, and all the other types of destruction we create for short-term gain, you get irreversible, disastrous results. Or in the words of Dr. Guy Harvey of the Guy Harvey Ocean Foundation, "In 40 years, a fishery that was sustainable for thousands of years has been essentially wiped out."[10] Meaning our fishbowl is already toast, so we are whipping a dead horse.

19. Immature yellowfin tuna in Borneo. Photo by Mark Spitzer.

Anyhow, whether we can reframe the actual catastrophic state of our oceans into an effective state of denial or not, that ghostly trawler—that spectral symbol of what we have wrought—vanished just as quickly as it appeared. Like boats vanish everywhere. Like species vanish everywhere. At a time when we don't have the time to be haunted. Because if we seriously want sustainable ecosystems, then we've got work to do Right Freaking Now!

Luckily, though, back at the dock there were a lot of stripers going on, which helped me reframe the indisputable loss I couldn't help acknowledging. Massive bass, most of them forty to fifty pounds, were being brought in by the wheelbarrow load. Their heads were the size of basketballs, and their immensity prompted me to reconsider a call I'd made in my last fish book: that striped bass are just too pretty to be thought of as grotesque.

Because these bass were true monsters! Healthy, strong, enduring monsters. Monsters off Montauk, where I got myself a trophy shark, then let it go, but kept a few realizations.

The first one being that it would be too easy to conclude with a platitude like "monster fish have a lot to teach us, but to learn from them we need to keep them around so that all their histories of crashes and regeneration can be allowed to render messages essential to their survival and our own."

Which is true, but of course there's something more. Something

20. Mike Smedley and Michael Smedley with Montauk
monster striper. Photo by Jonathan Smedley.

beyond the fact that shark and tuna need protecting, which everybody
knows. It was something deeper. Seriously! Something telling me that
I was heading in the right direction, but if this monster-fish thing is
really more than just an excuse for me to go fishing, then I need to look
even harder. Way harder! Which might not make for a tidy ending, but
that's where I found myself, standing on a dock at Montauk, opening a
brand new bucket of chum.

6

Monster Carp in France

In Pursuit of Fish without Borders

AS A KID FISHING ON THE MISSISSIPPI, I NEVER HAD ANY trouble understanding the primal thrill of hooking into a carp and horsing it to shore. But as an adult in pursuit of monster fish, I never understood the European craze of "driving and surviving" to catch what most Americans consider to be inedible trash fish. From England to France to Hungary and even Morocco, there's this obsessive culture of going after these massive, rubber-lipped bottom feeders using all sorts of high-tech gear costing thousands of dollars. That's why I made it my mission to get a handle on this mania.

The carp I saw online were girthy, barbeled behemoths, almost more vertical than horizontal. They weighed forty, fifty, sixty pounds—sometimes even a hundred—coming out of Spain, Germany, the Czech Republic, Croatia, the whole dang continent, where the common or German carp is indigenous. Though often believed to have originated in Asia, fossil finds show that German carp swam in the Danube at least ten thousand years before Christ. The Romans followed, farming carp for centuries on plantations. By the 1400s, carp were being raised in moats surrounding castles and in "stew ponds" by monks. A strong aquaculture commerce for carp was established throughout Europe in the Middle Ages, but as better-tasting fish like salmon and trout fell into fashion, carp became less popular. Then came the Industrial Revolution along with a need for sand and gravel pits to supply concrete and material for roads, homes, railways—infrastructure galore. By the time the 1990s rolled around, the carp now living in manmade lakes had grown into big fat fatties that far exceeded the twenty-pounders considered lunkers in the 1600s. Now, of course, super strains are being stocked, because what could be better than having an Incredible Hulkfish raging on the end of your line?

So almost six centuries after Joan of Arc sat down for a plate of carp, I chose Iktus for four main reasons: 1) It's in France, the geographical mecca of carp—especially for anglers from the United Kingdom who are absolutely bonkers for this fish; 2) Their two large lakes also have wels catfish topping 250 pounds, plus a wide variety of sturgeon, which grow fast and huge and make this fishery a novelty; 3) The facilities include a restaurant, a bar, a tackle shop, equipment rental, and cabins with electricity and Wi-Fi; and 4) Iktus has a variety of giant koi as well as grass carp. Hence, there were more than enough reasons to make arrangements through a UK outfit called Carp Fishing Trips. Also, the owner of that business, Rob Watts, offered to meet me at Iktus and personally train me on the dynamics of extreme carp angling—which was an offer I couldn't refuse.

When I got off the plane in Pau on the Spanish border, nestled at the base of the dramatic Mordor-looking Pyrenees Mountains, the first thing I heard was my name on the loudspeaker telling me to proceed to customer service. My checked luggage had been left in Paris, so they gave me a toothbrush and a plain white t-shirt along with some promises.

Rob, a cheerful bald Brit, was waiting for me with Jérémy Fournier, who resembled a wide-eyed Jim Nabors in his youth. Jérémy was the owner of Iktus, and without any further ado, we hopped into his Porsche SUV and shot on over to the lakes.

The presentation was impressive. The building overlooking the forty-acre lake was a stunning work of futuristic architecture. It housed a conference center, restaurant, tackle shop, and Jérémy's family's living quarters. A wedding was in progress, there were a bunch of cabins off to the left, and the parklike grounds were populated by joggers, bicyclists, horseback riders, dog-walkers, picnickers, and a pastoral herd of goats n' sheep. The water was a gorgeous, transparent jade color and full of sunfish, yellow perch, and plenty of plant life.

Rob took me to the bar for a beer, and then we hoofed it to the eighty-seven-acre lake along the picturesque River Pau. Our "swim" (or private fishing area) had two "bivvies" (or tents) already set up, and there were three twelve-foot rods on holders equipped with alarms. I had my brand new travel pole, a super-sturdy eight-foot Fox Sailfish rod, but my reel was in my lost luggage.

Rob sat me down and showed me the "shark rig" commonly used for carp, which operates on the logic that when a fish takes out line it can run freely. If the weight gets tangled on something, it's designed to snap off to protect the fish. The mainline was an ultra-durable fifteen-pound fluorocarbon, with a couple leaders on each pole made from twenty-pound sinking braid. The sections of line were connected by specialized swivels, stoppers, tubings, and knots.

My instruction came in an almost overwhelming rush. Rob showed me how to tie and connect and position the components of the rigs, and then I copied exactly what he did, taking notes as we went along. We covered knotless knots, overhang knots, Palomar knots, grinner knots, figure-8 knots, boilie needles, splice needles, fake maggot stoppers, gummy stoppers, multi-rig tools, blowback rigs, rig rings, hair rigs, bolt rigs, run rigs, death rigs, whippings, antitangle sleeves, tungsten tubings, tag ends, safety clips, aligning liners, and dissolving foam nuggets all on a sunny afternoon. The basic principal is that a "boilie," or prepackaged baitball, dangles from a hook attached to a "pop up," which is a marble-sized orb of foam meant to keep the bait floating about a foot off the bottom. When a carp sucks up the bait, it senses the metal, blows out what it just sucked up, and the hook gets caught on its inner-lip. It's then up to the angler to set the hook.

What I learned mostly from these lessons was that carp anglers take

2 1. Reverse snowman rig. Photo by Mark Spitzer.

their passion seriously, and they use a lot of gadgets as well. Some even use robotic bait boats that they send out to drop chum, which the British call "free offerings" or "freebies." Others use "spombs," which are bomb-shaped plastic casings that scatter freebies when you cast them out and they hit the water.

I must admit that the technical aspects of this sport were pretty intimidating to someone used to catching carp with just a few kernels of corn on a regular old hook. It was a lot of information to absorb in a couple hours, and it made me realize the sobering amount of detail this type of angling demands—a kind of attention which can only be compared to fly fishing. Plus, amateurs are not encouraged. If I didn't have professional guidance or proper tackle, not only would I be totally lost, I'd be endangering these fish. If I could even hook one, that is.

Rob's main advice to me was to always use the best boilies. Meaning the most expensive because they degrade less and stay on the hook longer. The boilies are also used as free offerings, so you don't want them to dissolve too fast.

Next, we went out in a rowboat equipped with a trolling motor, where we found a drop off with an echo sounder and deposited our bait along a ridge. We then threw out a few handfuls of corn and boilies and brought the rod back to the bait alarms. The line was set tight, and we made sure that the switch on the baitrunner reel was positioned in the "up" position. If it wasn't, we risked it being tugged into the drink.

After setting up the two other poles, Rob gave me some rig-tying homework and took off for a bit. I accomplished my tasks in enough time to take a walk along the bank through the clover and wild mint where I saw a nice-sized pike treading beneath an overhanging branch. That's what people fish for in the winter here.

Later that night, we went out for Mexican (not recommended in France), with a world-champ carp angler named Lee Merritt from the United Kingdom. An interview I'd recently read called Lee the "Mr. Nice of the carp world," and he lived up to this reputation by offering to help me in any way he could. He was accompanied by his no-B S girlfriend Joan from the North of England, where I was told the ladies give it to you straight.

Jérémy was there as well. I learned that he had earned two degrees, one in biology and the other in fishery management, and he had started his fishery ten years ago. I also learned that he had one paddlefish out there and a Ferrari. He said that if the airport called, he'd pick up my luggage. This left me wondering if it was appropriate to tip someone who drives a car worth more than my annual salary.

The evening continued with the fishermen showing each other photos of monster fish, and then Rob and I went back to our spot and "pub-chucked" the rigs out in the dark. We sat back in our camp chairs and

2 2. French guy and his forty-six-pound mirror carp. Photo by Mark Spitzer.

talked for a couple of hours. On the other side of the river, there was a festival going on. Fireworks began blasting the sky.

"Well," Rob said, after the first sonic boom exploded over the lake, "there go all our chances of catching a fish tonight."

And his words, unfortunately, held true.

But for the French guy in the adjacent swim, it was a totally different story. According to Rob, he had a better section of the lake, which is why he caught two catfish and two carp in the night. We were lucky for him to offer us coffee in the morning, and I was lucky to see his forty-six-pound whopper before he let it go.

It was a mirror carp, which is a genetic mutation of the common carp and a target fish of mine for this trip. They're rare in the states, but they're there. I caught one once in Missouri and hadn't known what to make of it. Mirror carp don't have uniform scales like commons do; they either have blobby calcium-like plates here and there or scattered scales, and the rest is slimy skin like a catfish. A variation on the mirror carp is the leather carp, which only has a few scales at the most and is extremely rare. The most famous is Heather the Leather, a fifty-year-old fifty-pounder who used to reside in Great Britain and is rumored to have been caught a thousand times.

The news then came that we could move to the VIP swim at the far end of that lake which would offer more possibilities. So we packed up our stuff and threw it in the Iktus truck, and within a couple hours we were set up on a gravel beach that offered a range of about 270 degrees of fishing off a spit where the big ones were breaching all afternoon.

But first we drove to the *supermarche* for some groceries, and when we got back to the tackle shop my bag had arrived. We grabbed that, I attached my Okuma 6500 Baitrunner reel, and then we had four rigs out in the lake.

Rob gave me some more knot-tying lessons, accompanied by some casting lessons I thought would never end. Still, these lessons proved to be invaluable because casting a carp rod isn't as simple as you'd think.

The sun went down and nothing bit, but occasionally a pesky muskrat crossed our lines, setting off an alarm. This proved to be a continuous annoyance for the rest of the trip.

I had made it a habit to sleep with all my clothes on (including wet shoes) in my sleeping bag to ensure the best chance of getting a carp. The alarm remote was clipped right over my ear on the headlamp that I also slept with, and it was always a rude awakening. That's how I slept for the whole week, jumping up and running to whatever rod was shrieking in the night. There were times, I think, that I didn't fully wake up until I found myself setting the hook.

I should mention that the line on the rods Iktus provided was floating line, which is why the muskrats kept setting them off, whereas the line on my rod was a sinking line that Rob had recommended. It was twenty-pound Halo P-line, and it stayed on the bottom, out of the way of trolling motor props and other swimming nuisances.

Then, around midnight, after several false alarms, I found myself cranking in a strange weight. It was like something was there, but it wasn't. When I got it up to shore, Rob declared it "A bloody bream!" Aka, *Abramis brama*, a carpy fish that had also been farmed in fishponds throughout the continent, of which Izaak Walton once remarked, "If he likes the water and air he will grow not only very large but as fat as a hog."[1] This one, though, was flat as a flounder, maybe four pounds, and I was glad to meet it. Rob, on the other hand, changed his original adjective to another one, since this meant that he had to go out in the boat and drop another rig where we'd dumped the freebies earlier.

But just as we were setting that rod back in its holder, another one went off. It was the rod and reel I'd trucked seven thousand miles, and I was on it in two seconds. I struck, and my pole arced.

"Easy, easy!" Rob advised, telling me to raise the rod and crank in while lowering down. "Gentle, gentle, keep its head up."

It was a carp alright, and that line was strong as hell. Unlike the carp I was used to playing in the states, this fish was pulling straight for the bottom. In the United States, carp are like torpedoes that rocket across a body of water and sometimes acrobatically leap, whereas this one relied more on strength and mass. It made a few runs, but I didn't allow it any slack. I let the drag wear it out, and then Rob met it with the landing net. Suddenly, I had the hugest carp I'd ever caught. It was a common, nearly forty inches long, and twenty-eight pounds!

Rob treated the puncture in its mouth with some blue first aid cream because these ain't run-of-the-mill rough fish that you throw on the bank to die; these are sport fish that you treat with respect so that others can enjoy them too. That's the norm, just like catch and release, and I wouldn't have it any other way.

It took a beer to settle my nerves, but I finally managed to get back to sleep. Nevertheless, the muskrats kept triggering the alarms, which kept on triggering mad dashes from my bivvy. At one point a fish hit,

23. Twenty-eight pounds, baby! Photo by Robert
Watts, www.carpfishingtrips.co.uk.

but when I yanked the rod out of its holder, a bird's nest erupted from the spool due to the ultrakinky line. When I tried to pull that tackle in by hand, it got snagged, and the line broke.

I bolted out of bed four more times that night and didn't get much sleep. What I did get, however, were photos to send to friends.

I also had Lee Merritt as a neighbor, who came over with nearly eighty pounds of carp in the morning. He had a thirty-eight-pound mirror and a thirty-six-pound common in mesh slings which he towed behind his boat. They were both beautiful fish.

I mentioned the term "drive and survive" earlier but without any explanation. This was what Lee and Joan were doing. As self-professed "Bus Wankers" (according to their bumper sticker), they often packed their van full of tents, fishing gear, bait, tackle, camp chairs, cots, bicycles, a grill, a propane-powered refrigerator, a DVD player, and all the supplies necessary to exist in a swim for a week—because nobody goes for less than a week. In fact, when I tried to book with some other lakes prior to finding Iktus, nobody would even return my emails when I asked for three or four days.

Rob and I then moved to Jérémy's private swim right beneath the tackle shop. Rob was flying back to the United Kingdom that day, and he figured that this swim would be an easier place for a rookie like me because of the deeper drop from the bank. The VIP swim had been really shallow, which made it hard to reach for the landing net when you're alone and twenty feet out in knee-deep water. Also, there were a lot less snags at Jérémy's private swim, which was on the smaller lake, also known as "the sturgeon lake."

Personally, I was glad to be closer to the restaurant that was hardly ever open, and the cabin I'd rented for the week, which had electricity, so I could charge my laptop and phone. It also had a shower and refrigerator, plus the aforementioned Wi-Fi, which would make life easier, even if easier wasn't the point. The point was to get to that still-elusive eureka moment that would elevate this whole monster-fish investigation into something worth a damn.

"Say," Rob asked, "can you bring the rowboat over?"

"Sure," I replied, but when I went over to the dock, it didn't have any oars in it. That's why I decided to lean over the bow and paddle with my hands, and that's how I saw them. They were hunkering under an overhanging willow tree, six eerily white ghost carp, some of them more than thirty pounds. I made a note of their spot and kept on paddling.

The next morning, after another night of muskrat harassment, false alarms, and a missed fish or two, one of the alarms started blaring. Sprinting out of bed, now on my own, I cocked the handle, hauled back, and it was on. It put up a noble fight, and when I got it to shore, it broke the misting surface with a blast of tangerine. Holy crap! Or holy carp, rather! It was a giant koi!

I netted it and got it onto the landing pad. What a fish! It only had scales along the spine, which meant it was of the Doitsu variety. But what struck me most was its human face. Though the eyes were standardly bulbous, there was an oval delineation within those orbs. That, coupled with the curling barbels resembling a neatly manicured moustache and the oblong contours of its head, conjured the visage of my Viennese grandfather, Herr Dr. Ernest Spitzer. That's who I saw, and he was clearly annoyed at being plucked from his environment.

Another way to look at it, however, was that I had just caught a seventeen-pound goldfish, which was a rare catch at Iktus or anywhere. These fish are reportedly very wary.

Anyhow, I got it into a sling then hung it on the side of the boat as I waited for the store to open so I could get someone to take photos. But since the store wouldn't open until nine o'clock, I ended up pacing the shore for an hour and a half. When I finally went up there, I found a cig-smoking Frenchie also waiting for the place to open. He said he'd be down in five minutes, so I ran down and held that brilliant orange fish in the sling, waiting for the guy to come down. Hell, I waited ten, fifteen, twenty minutes—and that bastard never came. Eventually, I went back up and got a shop guy to take the trophy shots.

And for the next three days, I didn't catch squat.

What I did catch was a better understanding of the culture of territory among carp anglers. Rob had told me about some sotted blokes who got mad at some Spanish fishermen for venturing into their turf, which is clearly marked on maps of the lakes. Those blokes then went over to the Spanish swim and got into some fisticuffs.

I experienced a bit of this tension as well when I looked up one day to see a Scottish fellow puttering right toward my floating line. I yelled at him, and he turned his boat around, but my hackles had been raised.

A few days later, scouting for carp around the island in my own boat, I guess I slipped out of my zone. When I was motoring back, I saw that

24. Spitzer and giant goldfish. Courtesy of Jérémy Fournier, Lake Iktus.

Scottish guy standing on the shore with his arms outstretched, which I assumed was the international gesture for "Big fish!" But as I found out ten minutes later when a bailiff came marching into my swim with the Scottish guy right behind him, what that gesture really meant was "WTF!?" I received a stern lecture about respecting boundaries, to which I replied with a thumbs up.

Here in the EU, there seems to be a lot of deeply rooted nationalistic consternation that goes back to other borders being crossed, both physical and metaphorical. For instance, I heard some complaints about Spanish fishermen being whiny and feeling entitled, some similar laments about the crassness of Dutch anglers, plus considerable talk about the borders that should be established for Muslims. Whereas some of these concerns are more recent than others, and whereas some go back to generations of warfare or even soccer grudges, there's no denying the fact that Europe (like the United States) is currently in the midst of a toxic debate about who belongs where and what should be done.

Similarly, the alarm-triggering muskrats kept crossing what I saw as my own borders, which is why I kept a pile of rocks by my chair. They, no doubt, probably felt the same way about me invading their lake, and we were having trouble finding resolution. But after a few days of yelling expletives and hurling stones, I realized that my bullying wasn't going to change their behavior, so I gave that method up.

Then, one afternoon, the goats n' sheep found a hole in the fence and got into my swim. Consequently, I found myself charging toward them and herding them away like a manic sheepdog. I didn't want them eating my bait, or the book I was reading, or maybe even my sleeping bag. A dog, also, once found its way in, as did a nosy cat that tried to get my smoked salmon.

That's when it hit me: whereas humans definitely have an awareness of borders, and whereas mammals understand them to an extent, carp aren't constrained by the lines we envision. In fact, we've been fighting such border crossings for decades in the United States, where in many places killing carp is either encouraged or the law. As a local news outlet in Salt Lake City recently reported:

> Crews are pointing to carp as the culprit for Utah Lake's brown water and lack of biodiversity. The fish first made their appearance in the 1800s, and now millions have taken over and the Utah Lake Commission is working to get most of them out of the water . . . to restore the lake and protect other species and plant life. . . . "Carp have been very destructive here in Utah Lake," said Mike Mills of the Utah Lake Commission. "Some people kind of refer to them as ecosystem engineers the way they feed, they cause a big change in the ecosystem. They root out aquatic vegetation, stir up nutrients, make the water a little less clear."[2]

Likewise, in Australia, there's a "carpageddon" going on in which millions have inundated the waterways of the Murray-Darling river system. According to an article in the *Telegraph*, authorities have been gearing up to use "a specially-developed strain of the (herpes) virus" to wipe out "a 'plague' of European carp."[3] At the time of this writing, action has not yet been taken, but when it does, residents will have to deal with 2,300 miles of rotting, reeking, rancid fish.

In France, however, right here right now, they're a desired species pursued for the exhilaration that comes with our sudden connection. And as food. Carp aquaculture has been in existence in China since at least 3500 BC, and there's still a huge commercial market in Eastern Europe where carp is traditionally served on Easter, Christmas, and New Year's. But on nonholidays, you can still find commercial carp regularly stocked in grocery stores and fish markets from Europe to Russia to Asia to the United States and beyond. In other words, all over the ding-dang world.

But as I considered all this, a frustration arose in stalking the ever-elusive great white koi. For several days I tried not to spook those wily ghost carps lounging in the shade on hot afternoons. I rigged up a pop bottle float to dangle some corn a foot beneath the surface and freebied that area constantly, but I couldn't get them to take the bait.

Lee and others figured that the overall lack of action was due to the stagnant weather. When it's hot and still, the fish don't move around much. But it wasn't always hot and still, and I saw plenty of fish moving around. I even saw a snaky sturgeon swim beneath my boat once, and they were always leaping in the middle of the lake. But for the most part, nobody was catching anything, not even Derek Ritchie, another world-class carp star staying on the lake. He'd caught a fifty-pounder a few days before, but that's when everyone else was catching them.

Anyway, somewhere along the line, it struck me that the word "self-ish" contained the word "fish." For a few fishless days I'd been trying to work this idea into the narrative I was drafting, which at that point wasn't feeling very optimistic. For literary purposes, I knew I could spin the story to make it seem like a recent chain of interconnected

25. Bon appétit! Photo by Mark Spitzer.

events was conspiring against me, but that just wasn't honest. Sure, I was battling rogue muskrats and renegade sheep, and I broke my stupid reading glasses, but I knew I wasn't diseased or eating dirt—so why complain? What I was was lucky to be drinking wine at night with very few mosquitoes out, and the sandwiches I was surviving on were some of the best I'd ever had (especially the green ones made with fresh avocado on country bread topped with pesto gouda). More to the point, I was in France, and fortunate to be doing what I loved, fish or no fish, borders be damned!

On another note altogether, despite all my observations about borders being crossed, I noted a lot of camaraderie. For instance, after three nights of not catching anything, I moved back to the VIP swim, where two other anglers stopped by on their bikes. They were making the rounds and talking to their neighbors to see if anyone was having luck. And the verdict, as previously mentioned, was that everyone was getting skunked.

26. Carp champ Lee Merritt with fifty-four-pound big momma carp at Iktus. Photo by Joan Batstone.

Everyone, that is, except for Lee, who had caught "a small one, about thirty pounds" two nights before, and a thirty-six-pound common the previous night, plus a monstrous fifty-four-pound mirror. In fact, he'd caught one in the mid-thirties that very morning, and when I was setting out my lines that evening I saw him fighting a fish from his boat so motored over just in time to see him land a forty-three-pound common.

Luckily for me, I now had Lee as my next-door neighbor again, and he just kept giving me stuff. His sponsors had stocked him with products to promote, so he gave me a bunch of High Impact carp boilies. He also gave me a spare pair of reading glasses, some weights, and insect repellent. But most importantly, he saw a fellow fisherman continuously getting burned, and he gave me what he could to remedy the situation. And all I could give him in return was lunch at KFC.

After I struck out four nights in a row, Lee came over with a bunch of tooty-fruity-smelling baits and four new rigs he'd tied for me. These rigs were a bit different than the ones I'd been using, mostly in that the pop up was the bait itself, which was screwed onto a short post extending from the curve of the hook. Not only that, but he found a problem with a linkage in one of my lines, fixed that, and advised going out in the boat to bring fish in.

"I don't take any chances, mate," he told me. "It's the best way to avoid the snags."

Then came the thunderstorm, which sucked for a bit because I had to sit in my bivvy not fishing. But when it abated, I lit out in the light rain, scanning for fish with the echo sounder at twenty feet, which is where Lee said they were biting. When I found a large mass, I'd drop in my rigs and throw out some corn, followed by a few handfuls of the candied boilies.

Since there weren't too many snags within fifty yards of my swim, I wasn't too concerned about getting hung up when hauling fish in from shore. But after I dropped my second line, I realized that I was 150 yards out. Since I'd already dumped the freebies, it would be a waste to relocate, so I decided that because there could be snags somewhere in all that space, I'd venture out in the boat if that particular alarm went off.

As usual, the sun went down. I drank a bottle of wine, then passed out on my cot. Alarms went off a few times, and a few times I jumped up. Each time, it was the dreaded amber light, the one I didn't want to deal with. Fortunately, they were all false alarms, either triggered by muskrats or passing fish.

But at 12:30 in the morning, the remote control clipped to my headlamp screamed into my ear, and this time it was long and constant. Holy hell! I leapt out of bed so fast that the elastic band around my head couldn't keep up with me. It blew off like a cartoon character who leaves his hat in a cloud of dust, and I wasn't going back to pick it up. I grabbed that pole, cranked the reel, hauled back, and it was Fish On!

The next thing I knew, I was out in the boat. It was swimming off to the left, making for the only dead tree sticking out of the lake. It was towing the boat, and I was doing all I could to keep my cool. To add to the confusion, it was pitch black, and I had no light. I couldn't even see it when I got it up next to the rail. All I saw was a bunch of silver splashery, but I finally led it into the net.

It was one of the most epic fish battles I'd ever fought, but I couldn't see what I had. So switching on the trolling motor, I hummed back to shore, where I lugged it over to the landing mat and retrieved my headlamp. I could now see that it was a common, and the exact same size as the one I'd caught before.

A few selfies with fish later, I applied some first aid cream to its abrasions, then let it go. My losing streak was over, and I couldn't have been more excited. I hadn't met my goal of bagging a mirror, yet I was satisfied enough to end the story right there.

But three hours later, another alarm went off. This time it was my own rod and reel, which handled like a dream. The fish made a couple runs, testing the drag, but I brought it in and was able to walk it back to the net then wade deeper out. I netted it, and the first thing I noticed was its prominent hunchback. Then I saw its glimmery skin. It was a mirror so devoid of scales that it bordered on a leather. It was a twenty-nine-pounder, and by gum, it was a bonus!

I saved that carp in the sling and somehow managed to get back to sleep. In the morning, after catching a twenty-five and a forty-four, Lee came over and took some pictures of my fish and me. And let me tell you: that carp was full of piss and vinegar! I could hardly hold it.

"So my tactics worked for you?" Lee asked after I released it.

"That and the bait made all the difference," I told him, forgetting that the rain had stirred them up as well. Then I added, "But I won't give all your secrets away."

Lee claimed there weren't any secrets, but I can think of a few details that I purposely left out because there's got to be some mystery. But even if there aren't any secrets, there's the fact that Lee is an international carping champ for a reason. When he drove off that morning, he left Iktus with ten carp under his belt amassing no less than 350 pounds.

After that, it was all downhill, but not in the unfortunate sense. I'm talking more like an easy ride. I was moved to a way less fruitful swim, where again I battled free-roaming livestock and trespassing rats and didn't catch jack. That, however, didn't matter. Nor did the fact that I never got a ghost carp. I'd gotten what I'd come to get, and even though

27. Fishin' mission accomplished. Photo by Lee Merritt.

I didn't catch a forty-plus-pounder, I witnessed two and can confirm that there are even larger fish out there.

Ultimately, I was left with two main conclusions:

The first was the obvious observation that it's a blast to go after monster carp, a fish which knows no borders—which are concepts we create for others to protect us from ourselves.

And secondly, since our fisheries were still in danger, it was time to get to the nutmeat of the matter. Meaning no more dicking around.

7

Bananas for Tarpon

A Matter of Timing in the Gambia and Beyond

I HAD A SCORE TO SETTLE WITH A MONSTROUS, HARD-HITTING sport fish. Tarpon had beaten me twice, and this time it was serious. The first time was on the river border between Nicaragua and Costa Rica, where trolling giant Rapalas, I hooked a six-foot-plus, 130-pound leviathan that leapt ten feet into the air. After a forty-five-minute back-breaking battle, I brought it up to the boat and my guide touched the leader right when the hook popped out of its mouth. According to IGFA rules I caught that fish, but since I didn't even touch it, I can't honestly count that as legitimate. And the second time was in Mexico, casting lures for juveniles. I had ten on in one day, but they were so scrappy that I couldn't bring one in.

Heading to West Africa in October, I figured, would put me in a good position to end this maddening grudge match that had been going on for years, and African Angling looked like the solution. Their website states, "Tarpon are by far the most powerful game fish of The Gambia. These extraordinary fish can . . . be targeted using a variety of fishing methods. The weight of a tarpon in The Gambia can range from 15lb to 250lb, with numerous fish having been caught over 100lbs and our largest standing at 303lbs."[1] And since that three-hundred-pounder was the unofficial world record, and since British expat Mark Longster had been connecting folks with this legendary fighter for over twenty years, the Gambia was the place to go.

But I had an opportunity to double dip as well. Stingrays could also be caught, so why not go for this prehistoric, alien-looking bizarro fish? African Angling was experienced in bringing in supersized stingrays, so it was on!

After trusting a shifty stranger with our passports at the Banjul Airport, scoring thousands of Gambian dollars on the black market, going in and out of stark rooms with armed soldiers, and paying off guides in the middle of the night, we caught a ride in a limping, coughing, cracked-windshield taxi with no headlights and made our way through multiple machine-gun checkpoints. There were abandoned shells of buildings on both sides of the highway, lost souls pleading for rides, and eerie blacked-out skies that made me wonder what would happen if the tranny dropped out on the road. Our driver, however, ground through the gears, we inhaled enough carbon monoxide to knock out an elephant, and we finally made it to the Senegambia Beach Hotel.

This exotic, whacko tourist compound for Dutch families and dirty old men paying for companionship was basically a cross between a snake farm and a luxury golf course. Monkeys and monitor lizards ran wild; there were half-feral, cross-eyed cats chilling all over; vultures hunkered in the palms; and crazy-colored, long-tailed birds were pecking on the lawns. Because it was four in the morning, we didn't see all this when we came in, but over the next few days we did—along with various models of sunburned vacationers lounging around the swimming pool, African dancers actually lighting their junk on fire, and the consistently exuberant English-speaking locals you couldn't help meeting every three steps, then end up repeating obligatory information to because we were on "The Smiling Coast," where, as the T-shirts say, "It's Nice to Be Nice."

After two days of exploring the beaches and trying out the local cuisine, "Bosslady" (as the locals referred to Lea) and "Bossman" (as they referred to me) were in a taxi heading to Denton Bridge. The sun was bright, the colors were brilliant, and the people swarming through the market shacks were hardly as intimidating as the night we arrived. In fact, we had fallen in love with the upbeat peacefulness of this war-free, storm-free country.

Our captain, Farmara, a silent yet jovial veteran of the Gambia River and the outlying coast, had been guiding for tarpon and stingray for twenty-two years. The first thing he showed us when we boarded the open-deck fiberglass boat was the cooler. He opened it, pulled out a bunch of bananas, and asked me if I wanted to leave them behind.

"Why?" I asked.

"Some fishermen don't like banana," he replied. "They say bad luck. One fisherman, he threw all banana overboard."

Bosslady and I laughed at that.

"If we don't catch any fish today," I said, "maybe we'll leave them on shore tomorrow."

Out on the ocean, it was a hell-ride to the stingray spot, jumping waves on the incoming tide. Bosslady and I were seated on a cooler which kept slamming our asses every time the boat slapped down. But we made it there and anchored up. The waves were still pretty rough, rising and dropping six feet at a time and tossing the boat from side to side. Let's just say that Bosslady wasn't feeling 100 percent excellent.

Farmara, meanwhile, baited up some heavy-duty Ugly Stiks with a fish called "bunga." The poles were equipped with solid surf-fishing reels and "extra huge" baitcasters. Some had ultrathick line in the one-hundred-pound range, others had woven line that looked to be around fifty- or sixty-pound test. I tried to get some specific information, but as noted before, Farmara was pretty much a silent guy.

Anyway, we put those baits on the bottom for the "batoids," an ichthyo-term that refers to skates, rays, stingrays, the whole weird-looking superorder of the family *Batoidea*. They're infamous, of course, for killing Steve Irwin, "the Crocodile Hunter," with their whiplike, spear-tipped tails. Some species even zap their prey with electrical currents. They're found in both fresh and salt water, and new species are discovered every year.

We also had two lighter weight rods rigged with two hooks each. We baited these with shrimp and dropped them on the bottom. I immediately caught two angelfish, which look like larger versions of the tropical aquarium species. They had kissy faces and zebra stripes, and Farmara threw them into the hold.

Not too long after that, he hooked into a barracuda and handed his pole to me. It leapt once but came in easy, about twenty inches long and silvery with black racing stripes along the sides. I held it up for a photo, and to my surprise it didn't act out. I caught a larger one later, and it also stayed relatively calm, which was a far cry from the frenetic cudas I'd experienced in the Dominican Republic.

As the day went on I caught a multitude of other fish. There was a small fish called "big eye," which had a large comic eye and some electric saffron highlights to its fins (which we saved for bait), and a frequently recurring rock bass that Farmara called "wrass." I also caught a "baby snapper" (a four-pound, big-lipped grouper), and I spotted an injured permit circling on the surface, which Farmara gaffed right through its humpback. But the most interesting fish was the one called "doctor." It was a funny-looking dark brown fish with a neon tangerine oval near its tail where two backward-pointing spikes could pop out like switchblades on both sides, skewering anyone dumb enough to grab it there (which is how it got its name). All these fish went into the hold.

Gambian anglers, I was learning, don't waste anything. Their fisheries are basically strong, healthy, and diverse, so it doesn't make any economic sense to practice catch and release when they've got families to feed. Since it's common for men to have multiple kids with multiple wives, there's a lot of children that need to be fed.

Anyway, it was an incredibly hot day with the African sun brutally beating down. A torpid heaviness set in around one o'clock, and we began baking in the afternoon heat while Bosslady slept on the bow. With the boat still going up and down, it took more than just concentration to keep the line tight on the bottom as I rode the undulations, only nodding off a few times. Nevertheless, I held the pole tight just in case something hit. But nothing did. They just weren't biting.

28. Junior, Fabu, and Bossman. Photo by Lea Graham.

Eventually the sea calmed, and I saw an extraterrestrial squid swim by, plus a giant sea turtle rise and dive. But what I didn't see were stingrays.

So at three o'clock we went looking for tarpon. Not fishing for tarpon—just looking for them because we didn't have the right bait. We needed mullets, I was told, and we'd get them tomorrow.

To sum things up, we then drove around, didn't spot any tarpon, and went back to the dock without any of my targeted fish. But I wasn't disappointed because I'd gotten a better sense of the ecosystem I was working with, and I caught some cool fish in the process. Fish which we couldn't do anything with since we were staying in a hotel, but others could. So we gave those fish away.

The afternoon before, we'd met these "bumsters" on the beach, which is a term for relatively harmless guys who hassle and hustle for whatever they can get. Junior was a thirty-year-old kid with a

Rasta cap, and Fabu was equally as smiley and inviting, and they had a charming glaze-eyed quality about them that felt a bit Jamaican. But what really sold me on these guys was that they were fishermen and had shown me pictures to elicit business. I told them I was working with another outfit, but if they could catch a stingray, we'd stop by for lunch.

So now that Junior and Fabu had caught a few, we stopped by at the appointed time. They came rushing down the fine white sand and escorted us up to "the freedom tree," which provided shade in front of their place. A table had been set up there, and they brought out some beers. After that, it didn't take long for "the Marleys" to appear.

Needless to say, Bosslady and I had a fine time hanging out with these characters and exchanging stories. They showed us more pictures of fish, and I showed them some on my phone. We talked about mass shootings in the United States, and they told us about how the hotel we were staying in was owned by the Lebanese, as were a number of other businesses on "the Strip."

"At the Lebanese Hotel," Junior told us, "they try to keep the tourists inside. They give you a cock-and-bull story about how it's not safe to go on the beach. Then the tourists, they give all their business to the Lebanese and don't meet the real people."

Who, he explained, need our commerce more than the Lebanese. Which is something we'd heard from another bumster who'd helped me find a bank machine. Of course, we could see both sides of this double-edged sword. On one hand, the hotel took business away from the homegrown Gambians, but on the other, it provided steady employment for quite a few locals.

Whatever the case, Bosslady and I were getting out, and we were getting to know "the real people." Especially Junior and Fabu, who, I began to realize, might be good backup in case Farmara couldn't produce a stingray.

They also told us about a fishing tournament that happens every year. I'd read about this contest earlier and knew that there was a prize for the biggest fish, which was usually either a monster tarpon or a monster ray.

"Every year an Englishman wins," Junior said. "He's not even Gaaambian, maaan."

"I know who you're talking about," I replied. "That's whose outfit I'm fishing with."

"He's good," Fabu nodded. "Yaaa, he's good."

Another thing we talked about was the incredibly welcoming attitude of the Gambians. To make a stereotype, they basically lack that desperate quality that translates to harassment in other underdeveloped countries when it's obvious that you have resources they don't. Hence, we returned to the concept of "nice."

"Of course it's nice to be nice," I began rambling. "I mean, why would you want it any other way? Everyone knows it's lame to be bad . . . to have to see yourself in the mirror when you know you're treating others poorly. It's a marketing tactic, nice to be nice. But here's the T-shirt I envision: "It's Better to Live a Good Life Than a Sucky One.""

It was a simple statement, and not really that genius, but at that moment, we were yukking up a storm and enjoying each other's company. Junior may have used the term "brother from another mother" to try to connect with me down on the beach, and we were all aware of the social inequality we couldn't directly address, but at that moment, that's where we were: in the Gambia, feeling the love.

Then suddenly the stingrays arrived. Junior's sister had cooked two of them over an open fire, and they were served upside down, looking like a bunch of meaty mushroom with striated gills. Those were the rays of the rays, the ribby bones of the big wings on both sides, which are actually pectoral fins that their whole bodies conform to. It was served on a giant platter: fish on one side, white rice on the other.

Junior and Fabu left us with our meal, and we picked at it for a minute. Then I flipped the whole mass over, revealing the heads. Their eyeballs were staring at us, and the small curvy rays along the edges were curling up and busting through the fresh-cooked flesh. They'd been prepared with their skin on, there were tubular bones all over the place, but there were also patches of pure white sweetness to dig into.

And when we did, both our eyes went wide, our eyebrows arching in disbelief. This fish we were eating, it was fantastic! Beyond anything we could've imagined! The flavor, the savor, the subtle sauce! The way the hot sauce brought the taste and texture together! The satisfying sizzle it left on your tongue! Holy cow! We had hit it! This was the instant! We were Here and it was Now!

But back to the stingray, which had some very chickeny qualities. First, it was finger-licking good. Second, its consistency was similar, and it had that buttery sort of fattiness. So me: I found myself slurping that meat right off the bone, enjoying the gristle and ritual of working for my calories, not to mention the contrasting layers of dark and light meat. Bosslady, however, wasn't so into the gelatinous skin and cartilage. She went for the clean steaky hunks she flayed off the rays. And when we finished, we could feel a pleasing greasy radiation sweating through our pores, a sensation akin to that gluttonous afterglow which comes from gorging yourself on chicken wings—which is gross to some but glorious for the salivary carnivore.

In fact, I'll repeat that word "gorge" again because that's what I'd done. I binge-ate to the point of great, bloated ecstasy. So as we sat there on the beach, gorged immaculate in the shade of the freedom tree, some nearby drummers thumping rhythm into the air, I knew that our timing was on. It had been perfect. And as Junior put it, returning with another round of beers and drawing out the long, flat sound of his a's: "Yaaa maaan . . . Gaaaambia."

The second day out, Bosslady opting to visit the slave island of Kunta Kinteh, Farmara and I had live mullets, most of them between four and ten inches long. They were kept alive in a big blue tub, Farmara recycling a bucket of water every twenty minutes to keep up the oxygen.

We shot straight out to the stingray spot, the sea a bit calmer than the day before but pounding steadily away. The sun was also way more intense as we cast out our bait and got to work sensing the tension and keeping it constant, which I was getting pretty good at despite the swells lifting and dropping the boat.

We caught a pompano and a croaking frogfish. Other than that, the bite just wasn't on.

The afternoon came quickly, and soon we were roasting away. The wind died down, the sea leveled out, but the tide was too strong, and it was keeping our shrimp off the bottom.

Still, I didn't complain or suggest we move. Farmara knew what he was doing, and if a stingray hit, it would be massive.

So as the dullness of the doldrums set in, the ultraviolet rays of our hydrogen star sucking moisture from our brains, I found myself reflecting on the Thomas McGuane book I'd been reading on the plane: *The Longest Silence*. I was really impressed by his gorgeous literary prose, and I'd given considerable thought to a moment of perplexing playfulness when he ended an essay with a character asking, "What do you know about that!" I mean, there wasn't even a question mark. What a strange way to end an essay: by prompting readers to ask that question of themselves. Just posing any question at the end of any piece of writing makes readers go back and review what they've read— which, in turn, makes them active participants in what's being discussed. That's why I always tell my students to try to leave their readers with a question to consider—the trick being to put the question out there without a question mark.

That sort of stuff tends to confuse my students, but that's okay. We should be confused because confusion spawns deep introspection, like the type I was doing now. McGuane had written some other things that were also sticking in my craw, and I was searching for resolution. For instance, there's a lot I can agree with in the following passage, but there's also a moralistic tangent I'm trying to unpack: "The fisherman now is one who defies society, who rips lips, who drains the pool, who takes no prisoners, who is not to be confused with the sissy with the creel and the bamboo rod. Granted, he releases that which he catches—"[2]

Whoa, stop right there! Okay, I see what he's saying about being outside society and ripping lips, and I get the thing about draining the pool, but what does he mean by not taking prisoners? Fish prisoners? I don't know. What I do know, though, is that if catch and release qualifies someone as a "fisherman," then I have a problem with that. Because here in the Gambia, and in many other places in the world, some can't afford to *not* eat what they catch. That's why Farmara filled the hold the other day, and no eating-size fish went to waste. Not that I condone taking as much as you can get like I saw anglers doing in Nicaragua, but I've seen the poverty along the Gambian highways, and I'd been through villages where children sleep in open-air shacks with sewage in the streets. My point being: whether McGuane intended it or not, it seems judgmental to have food on the table and criticize those with less resources for eating what they catch.

Such reflections always bring me back to a pair of poems that have always held a lot of truck for me. The first one is "On the Coast Near Sausalito" by Robert Hass, in which he examines one of my favorite monster fish, "the cabezone, an ugly atavistic fish." I'd caught such a sculpin in Puget Sound when I was six. Mine was mongo-headed and Gothic-finned, and I couldn't help considering some of the same issues as Hass in sacrificing it for dinner. When my father lined his knife up with its brain, I thought the same thing Hass wrote: "But it's strange to kill / for the sudden feel of life." Then, after twenty years of seriously considering catch and release vs. killing and grilling, I came to understand his following lines: "The danger is / to moralize that strangeness." Those lines articulate an issue meat eaters have been dealing with for millennia, which is why the stanza ultimately ends, "Creature and creatures, / we stared down centuries."[3]

Galway Kinnell made a similar point in his poem "The Bear," which I love to teach. Especially at the moment when the hunter, having wounded the bear and tracking it, comes upon a pile of its bloody scat. And what does he do? He thrusts it in his mouth and gnashes it down. "Gross!" I express to my students, playing the Devil's advocate. "Why would he do that?" But they know, and they tell me. And their translation is essentially another version of the last four lines of that poem: "the rest of my days I spend / wandering: wondering / what, anyway, / was that sticky infusion, that rank flavor of blood, that poetry, by which I lived?"[4]

And now I'll contradict myself by moralizing, which is a danger I feel confident addressing: "that rank flavor of blood," that's our gut questioning whether it's right to digest what we've taken. But the way I see it, eating an animal is a way of knowing it better. To have it in us makes it part of us, so putting it in us, that's about as sacred of an act as most of us can ever engage in. In a sense, that's the poetry by which I live—along with millions of others. And if you think about it too much, it leaves a rank taste in your mouth.

But guess what? We can eat our fish and have them too if we return to another premise proposed by McGuane: "We have reached the time in the life of the planet, and humanity's demands upon it, when every fisherman will have to be a riverkeeper, a steward of marine shallows, a watchman on the high seas. We are beyond having to put back what we have taken out. We must put back more than we take out."[5]

I therefore had a new question: what the hell can I put back?

The fishing that day didn't end well. After stewing in the sun all afternoon and not catching anything, we went inland on the Gambia River to the mouth of another river, where we anchored in the roiling, churning confluence. There were some shipyards nearby with guys repairing boats, and there were scattered wrecks here and there. On the flats in front of the oystered mangroves, there were ibises and storky birds high-stepping through the muck.

Farmara had heard that tarpon had been in this area the day before, so we were trying to time it right. We hung our mullets six feet beneath the floats, then again got to work just sitting there, watching the turbulent eddies swirling behind the outboard motor.

It didn't take long. A sudden tarpon rose next to us, and I saw its whole body flex. It was more than four feet long and at least fifty pounds. Then we saw two more rising side by side. They were smaller, but they were there. They just weren't interested.

I wasn't superstitious, but I couldn't help considering the bananas in the cooler. They hadn't contributed one dang bit to getting me a tarpon.

And since we weren't even eating them, it didn't make much sense to be driving them around.

But rather than chucking them into the river, I decided to take another approach. After two full days of no tarpon and no stingray, I wrote an email to the real Bossman. I told Mark Longster that I only had one day left and asked him if he could think of anything that would up my odds of getting a tarpon. I even stooped so low as to note that if he could hook me up, I could guarantee publicity.

Mark, in return, had written this back: "I have organized a new tactic for tomorrow . . . . Tarpon are around and can switch on any time . . . . sometimes it's down to a bit of timing."[6]

So on the third day, Bosslady opting to stay ashore, I took a taxi to Denton Bridge. I had no idea what the new tactic was, but when I stepped out of the cab I was told that "the boy" would be coming with us. Allegedly, the boy had caught four tarpon the other day and knew where they were.

Then I met the boy, who looked older than both Farmara and me put together. He had an ancient craggy face with barely three teeth in his mouth, but his shirtless torso was as lean as a teenager's. He introduced himself as "Ninja," and we boarded the boat, bananas and all.

"Now you have two captains," Ninja told me, but as he took the wheel and throttled out to the mouth of the river, it was clear who was piloting the craft. And when we got to the spot, right beneath an eroded terra-cotta cliff where the waves were breaking on the rocks and two different colored bottoms could be seen—one brown, the other dark blue—it was clear who was giving the orders on where to anchor. Ninja placed us right where the waves began to break, which lent to dramatic surges lifting us, followed by plunging drops felt in the gut.

The sea was definitely rough in that spot, but it was way less windy than the day before. A steel-gray mistiness permeated everything, and we put three lines in the water. The mullets started swimming out to sea, all following the same course, slowly towing their floats behind. When one got too far, we'd bring it in and cast it in on the shallower side.

We saw a few tarpon breaking the surface, and then one hit. Instinctively, I set the hook. The result was predictable.

"You got to let them take," Ninja said. "Just wait for *screeeeee*, then strike."

Given that, I decided to train myself to not set the hook. *If the line screams*, I kept telling myself, *don't do jack. If the line screams, don't do jack. If the line screams . . .*

Repeating this mantra in my head, I conditioned myself, I readied myself, I steeled myself for the hit. And when it came, I let that tarpon take out line.

"Should I hit it?" I asked.

"Yes! Yes!" both Farmara and Ninja shouted.

I hauled back, felt a nanosecond of resistance, and then absolutely nothing during the longest second of bafflement in my fishing existence. In the first half-second, the tarpon leapt: a beautiful, chromy, four-foot fish bending and twisting in the air. It shot five feet into the sky and looked right at us with its mouth agape. And as that happened, the reel spun free. Something was wrong. Like it wasn't locked, or the gears were slipping. But in the next half-second, as the fish slapped back, I cocked the reel, got it locked, and hauled back again.

Sometimes it's down to a bit of timing. Sometimes timing doesn't work. In this case, the rod arced. The fish was heading out to sea.

Ninja and Farmara scrambled. They got the anchor up and the engine going. And as the tarpon shot away from us, Ninja coached me, telling me to take it easy—which I was. He was telling me to reel in while lowering the rod—which, having been in this situation before, I was. And that tarpon, it was hooked good! It was hooked so damn good that I knew it couldn't get off.

It was a textbook battle. I kept horsing it in and wearing it out. For ten minutes straight, I fought that fish. Then it changed course and shot toward us, so I had to speed it up. It all came naturally, from fighting fish for forty-five years. Farmara got the net, and then Ninja groaned. The line was wrapped around a rock.

Farmara swore, which I'd never seen him do before, but I could feel the tarpon on my line. We circled the rock, hoping to unwind the fish. Under the water, I could sense oysters clicking and ticking against the line, which kept coming loose, mussel by mussel, limpid by limpid, barnacle by barnacle. Until finally . . . I reeled in a severed line.

My captains were definitely pissed off. They were kicking themselves and slapping their heads. But me, I was buzzing and ready for more.

Making our way back to the spot, we anchored up and cast out again. Our floats formed a bobbing triangulation, and at one point a sixty-pounder rose right in the middle of it. A half hour after that, I saw one leap near one of our floats, then reverse itself in flight. It was flying backward, seemingly flipping us off. Ninja told us that he'd felt it nip his bait, so it must've gotten a taste of metal, which is why it leapt so spastically.

Then Farmara hooked one, and it got off. He swore again. The pressure was on.

An hour later, Ninja was about to bring in a float to change the bait when suddenly he saw it vanish. He took a chance and hit it before the line even squealed, and instantly that fish was on. It leapt, and we saw it clearly in the air. It was the exact same size as the one that got away, so now it was time for me to pick up where I left off.

Ninja handed me the rod and Farmara sprang for the anchor rope. We were after it, and this time we weren't going to let it get near the rocks.

I fought that baby for fifteen minutes. It kept taking out line, and I kept bringing it back.

"If it goes to the rocks," Ninja advised, "you need to make it want to go the other way."

Again, I knew this and was doing my best to steer it away. Then, when we got it up to the boat, it dove right beneath us, so I had to keep it away from the prop. At that point, I had some pretty convincing persuading to do.

It was a truly epic fight, but in the end, it flattened out on its side, and I brought it up alongside. Farmara slipped the net under it and hauled it in, and "the silver king" was finally mine! Yeee-hawww! Clasping hands in the air! High fives! Total Fish Victory!

It was four feet long and forty pounds, a stunning slab of muscled fish. Its megascales sported a mica-like abalone sheen glimmering turquoise along the spine and sparkling with hints of pink. It was staring up with one huge eye, which is why its Latin name *Megalops atlanticus* translates to "Atlantic big eye." Being predators who hunt by sight, that's what those orbs are for.

It surprised me then when my captains didn't throw it back. Tarpon are Redlisted as "Vulnerable," and the World Conservation Union estimates a 30 percent drop in global abundance.[7] This decline is due to overfishing, the altering of river systems, pesticides, pollution, habitat loss, and harvesting of juveniles that haven't reached spawning size. Also, according to the Florida Museum of Natural History, "*Tarpon* are slow-growing fish and do not obtain sexual maturity until reaching an age of 6–7 years and a length of about 4 feet."[8] That's how long this fish was.

At the time, I didn't know it was a borderline juvenile, but if I did, I don't think I could've condoned the feast they were saving it for. As I keep repeating in books like this, eliminating immature fish from the genepool is the opposite of sustainable.

Nonetheless, I was damn thrilled to have caught it.

Since the stingray hadn't worked out, I hired Junior and Fabu to take me out the next morning, and at nine I showed up on the beach.

It was a big communal production launching that patched-up motorboat. About ten Gambian boys wheeled it down on its trailer and dropped it into the surf. I got in, followed by Junior, and then Fabu and a guy named Daniel boarded. Fabu was in the stern, readying the forty-horse Yamaha, and Daniel was operating the wheel. We were waiting for a window in the waves, which were breaking at about five feet.

After a couple false starts, everyone started yelling. They were pushing us out, trying to beat a gnarly roller, and something was going wrong with a linkage in the engine. Someone was pounding on something with a rock and Fabu was instructing him. They finally got it at the last second, Fabu pulled the cord, the motor shot to life and gripped the

29. Finally got it! Photo by Captain Farmara, courtesy of African Angling.

ocean, and we shot forward right as the wave broke on the bow, our timing down to the split second.

Out by the reef, we anchored up, and the smoke started going around. They set me up with a well-worn rod double-hooked with shrimp. I got to work tight-lining, and the others threw out some handlines weighted with sparkplugs, plus a heavy-duty rod baited with bunga.

Having spent the last three days doing this exact type of fishing, I was totally prepared and ready to fish. In fact, I caught four fish right off the bat, before anyone else caught anything. Two were angelfish, and two were butterfish, which are these slimy, blubbery, purple polka-dotted grotesques with buck teeth that used to be despised by tourists who now can't get enough. They're easy to fillet, and they've got a good clean meat that the restaurants buy up like crazy. The locals call them "chicken of the sea," and there's definitely something hen-like about them flocking around on the bottom.

Then I caught a barracuda, which my guides were surprised to see. Usually they don't hit off shrimp on the bottom, but this one did. I also got what Farmara had called a "wrass," but these guys said was a black grouper.

So we fished and fished, but mostly, Daniel and I fished. Because Junior, he worked his way to the bow, then passed out in the sun. It had been a late night for him. And Fabu, he wasn't feeling very well. Something about a headache and too much JulBrew beer.

Anyway, I kept bringing in the butterfish, and we kept tossing my catches into the bow. I was impressing myself by impressing them, but soon my catches started decreasing and Daniel's started catching up. Not that it was a contest, but an hour later, the waves lifting us and dropping us, he left me in the dust.

This got me thinking about what makes a good angler. In the McGuane book I'd been reading it struck me as curious that he kept qualifying anglers as "good" and "bad." There was some commentary on what makes an angler fall into these categories, and I found myself wondering what drives anglers like McGuane to judge other anglers according to these simple extremes. For fishermen like Junior and Fabu, a good angler is probably one who brings back enough fish to feed the community, no matter how they're caught. For McGuane, I suspect that a good angler is someone who's technically adept enough to catch a fish by thinking like a fish, but then that fish must be released. Where these views converge, I think, is in McGuane's assessment that "Good anglers should lead useful lives, and useful lives are marked by struggle, and difficulty, and even pain."[9] Therefore, I extrapolated, it's a matter of utility, and a respect for that utility, that defines anglers as good or not.

Whatever the case, the boat kept rising and dropping, and the butterfish kept coming in, but no stingrays like Junior and Fabu had promised. Until suddenly the fish just stopped, which didn't stop Daniel and me from trying.

A comfortable silence had also set in. We were each in our own world, hunkered in our own spots, either asleep or nodding off. Junior was definitely out, and Fabu had wrapped himself in his own arms. He was shuddering like a junkie, trying to hold his sickness in. Neither of them were even trying to fish.

In my case, I had entered a strange limbo where I was leaning forward, keeping my line tight, elbows propped on my knees. It was easy to fall asleep and wake up and keep enough tension on the line. If the line twitched under my thumb, I would react. And Daniel, in the stern, was doing the same thing.

Basically, we were all a bunch of lumps—but it was nice. Nice to be out in the sun. Nice to be together not saying anything. Just fishermen fishing, despite our obvious dispositions and the fact that again my time was running out.

I was wondering if we should move to another spot, even though I knew that if I raised that question (and I did) they'd say we should stay where we were. Because moving to another spot, that's not always advantageous when you're trying to conserve gasoline. Also, taking your bait out of the water, then taking time to motor somewhere and re-anchor, can often translate into less fish. So I understood why we were there.

The truth, I finally had to admit, was that we were out there to catch food, and they were using me to add to their supply. To them, it didn't really matter if I wanted stingray. One might come along, and that would be fun, but in the meantime, we were going to catch as much as we could and not waste time bucking the odds.

But this didn't bother me because suddenly I was stung by the satori that I can't be disappointed if I don't get a stingray because this is what it's all about. It's about being on the water. It's about what happens along the way. It's about being excited about your goal, even when you can't stay awake. And it's also about being by yourself when you're with others. And when that's the case, it's sometimes about the cliché of being brothers bound by a passion, even when everyone's aware of the underlying business transaction.

I also knew that I didn't need a stingray because I'd already got the tarpon I'd come for. Sure, a stingray would've been a bonus. But more than that, it's a bonus to have an excuse to do what you love in order to have moments like this. And really, I want more moments like this—in which I realize that I've had my stingray all along.

Then, right at that moment, Fabu jerked, bolted straight up, and leaned over the rail. And timing it perfectly, he puked into the sea.

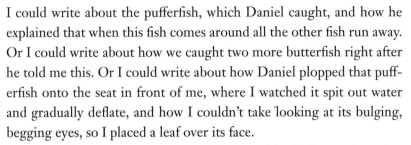

I could write about the pufferfish, which Daniel caught, and how he explained that when this fish comes around all the other fish run away. Or I could write about how we caught two more butterfish right after he told me this. Or I could write about how Daniel plopped that puff-erfish onto the seat in front of me, where I watched it spit out water and gradually deflate, and how I couldn't take looking at its bulging, begging eyes, so I placed a leaf over its face.

Nope, what I'm going to write about is suddenly discovering what I'd been looking for. Because there it was in my face: the missing link! The direction I'd been seeking! My hook in search of monster fish that was going to make everything fall into place!

But first we had to shoot in on the incoming tide, load the trailer, and haul it up the beach. Then it was trophy-shot time.

The fish we caught were laid on a plank. I knelt down in front of them, Junior joined me on my left, and Fabu slid in on my right. Someone handed me the barracuda, Junior exposed some beaveresque butterfish teeth, and Fabu showed off an angelfish. The whole community gathered around, the great-white-hunter pictures were taken, and as I stood up, calamity broke out.

Kids and mothers were scrambling for fish. Some shoulders came in and body-checked people aside. And for the first time in the Gambia, I heard dissent. Squabbling. Shaming. Even some smack talk.

"Why you get all the good fish!?" I heard someone ask, only to look over and see Junior and Fabu walking away with the barracuda and the three fattest butterfish.

People were definitely annoyed at them, but Junior and Fabu, they didn't give a damn. They just motioned for me to follow them. And as

I paid them their seventy bucks, I could literally feel something akin to a hissing behind us.

But what really matters is the epiphany McGuane had led me to: it was the question of putting back more than we take out. Because here we are, and our ecosystems are going down, and as McGuane pointed out, we're *beyond* needing to put back—a fact documented by thousands of scientists who've reached consensus on global warming. Because technically, it is too late. Our ship is sinking. Meaning patchwork is our only hope.

That's the conundrum of timing. It takes a lot of foresight to get things right, and it takes a lot of convincing to make both fish and people change directions. In essence, we are a species that looks out for ourselves first, and if tarpon have to pay the price for the sins of the industrialized world and hunger in developing countries, so be it. That's our attitude, and that's the creed by which we live.

But on the flip side, it's not like we're guaranteed more than a century on this planet anyway. As I've been pointing out, at the rate we're going, we won't have any ice caps left in a century. Add to that the reality that we are past the tipping point of a pH level of 7.8, plus the fact that all that melting ice contains carbon that can evaporate as methane, which is almost thirty-five times more powerful than carbon dioxide in veiling the atmosphere with greenhouse gasses, and we get David Wallace-Wells's apocalyptic warning from *New York Magazine*: "we have, trapped in Arctic permafrost, twice as much carbon as is currently wrecking the atmosphere of the planet, all of it scheduled to be released at a date that keeps getting moved up, partially in the form of a gas that multiplies its warming power 86 times over."[10] Wallace-Wells expects such heat to come stock with severe drought, phenomenal floods, dire diseases, imminent crashes in world crops and the human immune system, terrifying plagues of insects, debilitating ozone smog, and mass die-offs of marine life from ocean acidification. And as the journal *Geophysical Research Letters* points out, there are also 32 million gallons of mercury, which is "a potent neurotoxin and serious threat to human health," thawing out in the Arctic right now.[11]

Still, it doesn't have to be that way because we can try to slow our slide. How? By actually envisioning the monstrous results we can't bear to imagine. That is, we need to face the damage we're doing with the intensity of those cigarette packages that show graphic images of blackened lesions and infected gums. Because looking away from what we're doing, refusing to register the consequences of our actions, that's just suicide.

But back to what I'd been searching for, which in effect had just found me: the slap-in-the-face realization that since it's physically and economically impossible to put back more than we take out, we can only give back in other ways.

But here's the trouble: it takes activity. As in action. As in "activism," which is admittedly a scary word; but a word that doesn't have to be scary if you find what drives you and apply it. Like those, right now, studying biology, ecology, and more eco-friendly management practices. Like those who are running for office in order to make policy changes from the inside. Like those who are marching in the streets or knocking on doors or making phone calls. Like those who are spreading the word through music, poetry, video—whatever means possible. And like those who don't know what to do, so they're trying to learn, or they're just walking around wondering what the hell to connect with—which is an active form of being lost, and the world needs more of that. Because most of us, we feel too powerless to try to do anything—which is what makes us believe we can't.

So that's where I was, stymied on the Gambian sand, gulls squawking in the sky. They were asking me why I shouldn't continue to fish and preach and catch and release and eat some fish on this planet, where a bit of timing can make all the difference in getting a tarpon or delaying the unthinkable.

And I, now armed with what I needed, was ready to get down to business.

8

Striking Gold in Senegal

One Monster Fish Leads to Another

SETTING OFF FROM DAKAR IN A STURDY THIRTY-FOOT CRAFT powered by a 225-horsepower outboard, Issa wove us in and out of the incoming rollers. The waves were ten feet tall and crashing down in roaring foam, and we had to beat them before they beat us, which was no problem. Denna, the first mate, also Senegalese, clung to the canopy frame, as did I, the entire Atlantic opening up before us just as sapphire as the sky.

We went about half a mile, then came to a fishing boat which I can only describe as an oversized pirogue of the typical model used in West Africa. It was made entirely from wood, painted a lot of bright colors, and banana-shaped. There were about ten fishermen in this one, of which half were boys between the ages of eight and eleven. They were pulling in a net in which they'd corralled their quarry, and the diameter of the encircling floats was decreasing with every tug.

We pulled up as they hauled in about twenty silvery white ballyhoos, a Pinocchio-looking baitfish I recalled from the Caribbean. They were a foot long, and a dozen went into our bait cooler. A shouting match then ensued between their captain and ours with people on board the other boat restraining the irate fisherman. I couldn't tell what was being said because they were speaking a mixture of French and Wolof.

Meanwhile, there were smaller pirogues zooming up and down the waves like a swarm of hornets going every which way. Most boats were propelled by 15 hp two-strokes, and each one was occupied by a single fisherman steering in the stern while trailing a handline. There must've been about forty of these boats expertly avoiding each other as they circled an area that was obviously rich in fish.

They were out there for small tuna, a foot long each, and when they hooked one it was a phenomenal sight. Working their arms above their heads, strips of cloth wrapped around their thumbs, they pulled the cartwheeling tunas in. Then, in one single motion they'd unhook their catches and toss them forward while veering away from oncoming boats.

I couldn't help it. In my head, I labeled these guys "the X-wing fighters."

When I came to Dakar, I had no idea what I'd be fishing for. We'd made reservations to stay at this place called La Cabane du Pêcheur, which was right on the shore and connected to a fishing charter service called Atlantic Evasion. We ate prawns and oysters in their bar and watched boys doing pushups on Ngor Beach while women with baskets on their heads sold bracelets and dolls and hippo carvings to the few tourists out on the October sand. There was a red monkey with a long expressive face shackled to a pile of trash by the front entrance which some locals tormented and others fed, and on the walls inside there were tarpon heads and tuna heads, but most of all, the heads of giant swordfish.

It was a fish I knew nothing about, but a fish I had on my monster list because of that spear-shaped snout which has actually skewered dudes. I'd seen an interview on TV about one that had leapt into a boat and stabbed a kid right through the face, and I had read of some incidents too. Swordfish have been known to attack boats, sometimes even sinking them by piercing holes right through hulls. If that doesn't qualify a fish as monstrous, then I don't know what does.

Those saber-schnozzes, by the way, are made from bone and cartilage and are used to stun smaller fish. When swordfish go bursting into schools and slashing all around, they wound their prey, then come back and swallow them.

Anyway, I figured that the fishing trip I booked was reef fishing for small fish. But the next day, when I found out that it was an excursion for blue marlin, my whole world instantly flipped.

I immediately started researching and found out that "swordfish" is a blanket term for any fish with a swordlike upper-jaw, but it's also a specific species, *Xiphias gladius*. According to Wikipedia, a source I tell my students to avoid, the blue marlin is a member of the billfish family, which consists of sailfish (*Istiophoridae* family), marlins (same family), and swordfish.[1] More importantly, because blue marlin can reach sixteen feet and weigh a ton and leap fifteen feet, they're often considered "the holy grail of fishing."

As for the species' place in literary history, I was reminded of the role the marlin played in Hemingway's *Old Man and the Sea*. But for some reason, I was more intrigued by its connection to a popular western author I had never read.

Zane Grey was a fishing fanatic, and he went after billfish all over the planet. He held multiple world records, was the president of a few exclusive fishing clubs, and according to his son, spent three hundred days a year fishing in his later life. He actually pioneered the sport of sailfishing, and was also the inventor of a hookless lure called "the teaser." He caught the first thousand-pound fish on record for rod and reel and wrote numerous nonfiction articles for outdoor magazines.

In his 1919 book *Tales of Fishes*, Grey includes a chapter entitled "From Records of the New York Bureau of Fisheries, by G. B. Goode." This excerpt weighs in on the confusion regarding the difference between swordfish and sailfish and marlin, in which the ichthyologist declares "spear-fish is a much better name" for the whole genera.[2]

In order to provide an idea of the swordfish's raw strength, Grey then uses Goode's account of a Professor Richard Owen, who testifies "in an England court in regard to [this fish's] power." I have no idea why a billfish was on trial, but this is what went down in the book: "It strikes with the accumulated force of fifteen double-handed hammers.

Its velocity is equal to that of a swivel shot, and is as dangerous in its effect as a heavy artillery projectile."[3]

That chapter also includes a short history of fishing for swordfish with spears. No doubt, this is where Grey's inspiration to harpoon dolphins came from, which is why he cofounded a club circa 1912 for the express purpose of porpoise hunting. Flipper, beware!

One particular paragraph, however, deserves its own time in the spotlight again for the mythology it provokes. It covers a vast range of subject matter, including sportfishing, rumors of attacking vessels, and the PTSD swordfish are capable of afflicting fishermen with:

> The pursuit of the swordfish is much more exciting than ordinary fishing, for it resembles the hunting of large animals upon the land and partakes more of the nature of the chase. There is no slow and careful baiting and patient waiting, and no disappointment caused by the accidental capture of worthless "bait-stealers." The game is seen and followed, and outwitted by wary tactics, and killed by strength of arm and skill. The swordfish is a powerful antagonist sometimes, and sends his pursuers' vessel into harbor leaking, and almost sinking, from injuries he has inflicted. I have known a vessel to be struck by wounded swordfish as many as twenty times in a season. There is even the spice of personal danger to savor the chase, for the men are occasionally wounded by the infuriated fish. One of Captain Ashby's crew was severely wounded by a swordfish which thrust his beak through the oak floor of a boat on which he was standing, and penetrated about two inches in his naked heel. The strange fascination draws men to this pursuit when they have once learned its charms. An old swordfish fisherman, who had followed the pursuit for twenty years, told me that when he was on the cruising-ground, he fished all night in his dreams, and that many a time he has rubbed the skin off his knuckles by striking them against the ceiling of his bunk when he raised his arms to thrust the harpoon into visionary monster swordfishes.[4]

Here's another moment from that chapter that says a lot about this fish's spirit:

When the fish has swallowed the hook it rises to the surface, making prodigious leaps and plunges. At last it is dragged to the boat, secured with a boat-hook, and beaten to death before it is hauled on board. Such fishing is not without danger, for the spear-fish sometimes rushes upon the boat, drowning the fisherman, or wounding him with its terrible weapon. The fish becomes furious at the appearance of sharks, which are its natural enemies. They engage in violent combats, and when the spear-fish is attached to the fisherman's line it often receives frightful wounds from the adversaries.[5]

The bottom line being, with reports such as this, I was more than just psyched to get myself a legendary blue marlin. If anything, I was a kid again, pumped up with childlike wonder, visions of marlins leaping through my head.

We set out trolling with the four biggest baitcasting reels I had ever used in my life. They were gold Shimanos, each the size of a gallon jug, and they were strung up with some incredibly thick polymer line. The two outside rods were connected to outrigger poles that stuck out like alien antennae, almost twenty feet long each, and they were equipped with rubber bands that would snap if a fish hit, causing the lines to whip out in the wake of the boat. The idea being that with two lines on the outside and two lines over the stern, these arms would keep tackle from crossing each other and tangling up.

Trailing behind us, I could see two de-nosed ballyhoos skipping over the surface at roughly twenty yards, and two sparkling squiddy lures that must've been fifteen inches long skimming the surface fifty yards out. The ballyhoos had giant circle hooks strung through them, and the lures were equally as formidable.

Getting to the spot took almost an hour. It was twenty-five miles away, and on the way we saw flying fish just brushing the waves. At first I thought they were birds because of their gliding flappery that lasted up to forty yards. But sometimes, they'd push off on the crest of a wave and gather another ten or twenty before returning to the sea.

I tried to ask my "English-speaking crew" about these fish, but their English was worse than my French, which was only sufficient for exchanging cursory information. This made it difficult to get a handle on tactics.

As usual I was taking notes, writing down the details I saw. Like the bright orange buoy we eventually came upon marking the fishing grounds. There were gulls diving and more flying fish, plus occasional bursts of small tuna here and there due to larger fish forcing them up. It was all going on within a half-mile radius of the buoy, which was being circumnavigated by another swarm of the aforementioned X-wing fighters.

I took a closer look at their pirogues, which tended to have names like "Papa This" and "Papa That" painted on the sides. Other names were written in the national language (as opposed to the language imposed by the colonial power), and some pirogues were decorated with portraits of people. Some of these were of Muslim-robed elders, but others were of infants in their swaddlings. Also, many of the outboard motors were decorated with patchworks of different colored fabrics that left me scratching my head. Were these purely ornamental, or were they sewn by wives for good luck, or did they serve a utilitarian purpose like keeping the metal from heating up in the sun?

I couldn't tell, but I could see the arms of the fishermen working like windmills to pull in the tuna they tossed up front. Other times, they bailed out bloody water, which consistently collected in the stern since the bows were always pointing skyward and the spray kept coming in and washing down through the fish.

There were about thirty swooping, veering, multi-tasking X-wing fishermen tearing around in that spot, and each of them was bringing in tuna every few minutes. At this rate, I estimated that if each boat ended up with two hundred fish at the end of the day, then at least six thousand tuna were harvested daily from this spot.

It was an active and impressive vision, but ultimately disturbing. The other day I'd walked through the fishing village by our hotel, and I'd seen baskets of tuna being sold in the labyrinthine alleyways. The average size was a foot long, and I later asked a fishing guide what kind of fish those were. She told me they were yellowfin (*Thunnus albacares*), which is known as "albacore" in French. "Albacore," however, is a deceiving word because albacore tuna (*Thunnus alalunga*) is an entirely different species.

Anyhow, because of that misunderstanding, I was under the impression that the X-wingers were mass harvesting sexually immature yellowfin tuna which reproduce at about twenty-one inches. What I was really watching, though, was the mass harvesting of skipjack tuna (*Katsuwonus pelamis*), which reproduce at nearly sixteen inches. But it didn't matter that my species were mixed up because none of those fish were measuring up to spawning size. The fact is that when you take juveniles out of a system, it stunts the whole damn food chain.

Hence, it wasn't just a small percentage of the overall commercial fishery taking place off the Senegal coast that I saw being boated; what I was witnessing was an actual sample of what's happening all over the overfished world. Of course, habitat loss and pollution and other factors work into the grand equation, but if there's one thing I keep learning from studying fisheries it's that world tuna populations are being devastated at a totally unstable rate. All populations have plummeted severely in the last half century, and as the WWF recently reported in the *Guardian*, global tuna and mackerel populations have suffered a catastrophic decline of 74 percent in the last forty years. The take-home message being: "We are destroying vital food sources, and the ecology of our oceans."[6]

But back to skipjack tuna, which is commonly canned and currently listed in the category of "Least Concern" by the IUCN.[7] This species accounts for 40 percent of the entire tuna industry. As noted in the article "Overfished Tuna 'Near Extinction,'" "Marine scientists have little idea how long [skipjack] will be able to withstand rising catches."[8] And as history has shown, when we become dependent on such heavily fished commercial industries like those of cod or sturgeon or salmon or bluefin tuna, demand eventually takes its toll in the form of drastic crashes. We then wait too long to establish regulations, illegal operations take place, and imminently, the well goes dry. After that, we move on to alternative species, and the cycle starts all over again.

Nevertheless, Denna casted out a chromy fly-like lure on a lighter rod and handed it to me, and following the zooming X-wing fighters, we hopped on the eradication bandwagon. I hooked a tuna instantly, and it skipped across our wake as I hauled it in. A few minutes later, I hooked another and brought it in as well.

Issa then took a knitting needle with a loop of string on it and poked it through a tuna eye. He penetrated its brain, slid it through the other eye, then pulled the loop through its spasming head. Securing the loop to a circle hook, the expiring fish was then ready to be used as bait, and I wasn't above playing a micropart in the destruction of this fishery. The other tuna was hooked as well, and we dropped them in, cut the engine, and began fishing for blue marlin.

Montage: alternating between trolling and drift fishing, we cast for tuna. Every fifteen minutes, we'd reel in the bait and switch it. Freshies were necessary, which meant that we—like hundreds of other sportfishers doing the same thing at the same time worldwide—were contributing to a decline in skipjack tuna.

And as the African sun blazed its way through the afternoon, the catching of bait became tougher and tougher. We started relying on one of the X-wing fighters who'd swoop by and toss us a live one whenever it was needed.

That's what we did for the rest of the day. We burned through about sixteen juveniles, and we didn't even get a bite.

But later, Issa was letting out some line, and he was intent on something deep beneath the surface. He then handed the rod to me and told me to reel in.

There was nothing on the other end, but apparently something had happened. When we got that tuna back to the boat, we saw a big slice on it. The thing is, when a big fish chomps a little fish, there's usually chomp marks on both sides. But on this fish, the injury was only on one side—meaning a marlin had slashed it with its razor-sharp beak, then decided not to go for it.

By five o'clock, my eyes were stinging from the salt air, and I was exhausted from the sun. Having only eaten a measly cheese sandwich I was also hungry, so I cut off a slice of tuna that I decided to think of as sashimi. In part, I did this to keep from feeling guilty about all

30. Marlin-slashed skipjack tuna. Photo by Mark Spitzer.

that skipjack going to waste. Still, any semblance of regret I might've entertained was overshadowed by a fog of frustration. I'd been pumped to catch a blue marlin, and now all those visions of bringing back a cobalt-blue ten-footer and hanging it from the winch in front of the hotel were basically smashed to dust.

But considering the conservation status of this fish, it's a good thing I didn't bring a marlin back. In the last fourteen years, blue marlin populations have declined 31 to 38 percent, and they're Redlisted as "Vulnerable." Much of this is due to being the unfortunate bycatch of the tuna-fishing industries, which rely on the practice of longlining, which leaves thousands of marlin dead on the line. As the IUCN also notes, "This species is not considered to be well managed in any part of its range."⁹

Just like us, I figured, trolling back to Ngor Beach with little confidence that a marlin would explode from the depths and tail-dance my eyeballs off. Apparently, Issa and Denna felt the same way because our trolling speed was pretty swift.

So I gave up. It was over. I knew it, and I was bummed—yet thrilled to know that I could still encounter what the French call "the blue emperor." This was all part of my new attitude, which I'd picked up while considering the stingray, so my emotions were admittedly both pessimistic and optimistic at the same time, and I was feeling the buzz and burn of both.

That's when we hit the dolphin field. One jumped and I saw its stereotypical silhouette hanging for a second above the water, and then it splashed down and I cheered. Sure, I'd seen plenty of leaping dolphins in my life, but this one came at a time when I needed something.

Then there were more. They were swimming toward us and under us, just a foot beneath the surface, and I was whooping up a storm.

And suddenly, with only a mile to go before the fishing trip was finished, something white appeared in the direction the dolphins were heading. It looked like a puffy marshmallow, so Issa changed course, and we followed the dolphins to see what it was.

It was a bloated, rotten, nasty-ass porpoise—just the front half. It was blubbery and stringy and decaying and rank with a spaghetti of arteries and tubes hanging from it. Its skull could be seen coming through the decomposing meat, its teeth exposed and curving along its jawline in a stomach-curdling, grimacing grin.

Swinging about, Issa turned to me with a toothy smile of his own and uttered a single word:

"Dorado."

Also known as mahi-mahi, dolphin, dolphinfish, and green dolphin, the dorado is a hydrocephalic-headed creature with a quasi-Quasimodo quality that makes it a mutant-looking fish. On the flip side, others see it as a stunning amalgamation of neon gold and aquamarine, so therefore a gorgeous fish. But that's the thing about monsters: they aren't always pure evil or pure ugly because they're eerier when there's a tension involving beauty. Because let's face it: monsters are paradoxes invented by paradoxes who can be just as terrifying as they can be alluring. Take the classic concept of sirens, for example, attracting sailors to their deaths. Or the statuesque centaurs of Greek mythology. Or sexy vampires. That's why I'd classify dorado as something freaky enough to be classified as "monstrous."

Consider also that the words "mahi-mahi" translate from Hawaiian as "super-duper strong," and that this species can be found grubbing out on putrid porpoises which no self-respecting salmon would touch with a ten-foot pole, and we've got even more reason to lump *Coryphaena hippurus* in this creepy club. Being carnivorous top predators (the Greek root of *koryphe* meaning "apex"), they also grow at an inhuman rate and become sexually mature before they're a year old. But most of all, they have those unearthly perverted faces complete with smooshed-in simian brows.

As for their range, they're in the tropics all over the world, but I had never met one before. I'd seen them caught by fishermen in the Caribbean, and I knew they were good to eat, but I'd never considered going for one. Now, however, I had the chance, so I was going to take it.

We got down-current of the foul-smelling porpoise, where Denna sliced some strips of the belly flesh off a tuna and Issa rigged up a lighter rod. Denna attached a bloody chunk and threw it out by the side of the boat and let it sink while I released line. Then Denna motioned for me to reel in.

Instantly, something was splashing on the water, and then it leapt. It was a technicolored dorado shining like candy, completely out of the water and shuddering as if charged with lightning. Its colors were crazily incandescent, and I saw it spit out my bait.

"Reel! Reel!" Denna yelled, so I powered down, burning that tuna chunk across the surface. The dorado was hot on its tail, hurdling in and out of the water. Then it connected again, the rod bowed, and the fish dove.

I horsed back and the dorado came up a few more times with some tremendous aerial acrobatics, somersaulting and corkscrewing and flipping in the air. I whooped, then got it up next to the boat. My guides motioned for me to let it wear itself out, so that's what I did. It swam around under us, and they told me to hold it there while they scrambled to get a handline baited. When they threw that line overboard, we turned our attention back to the fish thrashing beneath us. Denna gaffed it in the back and hauled it over the rail.

It was a vibrant five-pounder, but nobody stopped to check it out. A trap door was opened and the fish was kicked in so we could concentrate on the other line. Issa plunged the corpse of a chopped-up tuna into the water and started scrubbing it with a brush. Blood and chum were coming off as a dazzling pack of iridescent blurs passed like sharks beneath us.

Issa then baited my line and tossed it in and something took it straight away. I reeled in, and it was on. It came up at least four feet long and peeled off ten yards of line. I had to bring this one in by raising the pole, then reeling on the way down. The fish stayed down, but then it switched directions and shot straight into the sky.

Man! I ended up battling that dorado more in the air than in the water. It kept bursting up and shaking like an incensed bull, and I kept pulling its thrashing mass toward the boat, coaxing it back into the ocean. Fluming and spuming, it just kept erupting in front of us. I'd reel in while it was airborne, and it was going just as nuts as I was, yowling every time it leapt. It must've launched itself eight or ten times, the jumpingest fish I ever fought. But ultimately, I led it toward the boat and let it swim circles for five more minutes before Denna gaffed it.

Somewhere in that pandemonium, Issa hooked a smaller one on the handline, and we got that one in the boat as well. I then caught a third one, also smaller, but can't remember any of the details—because really, it was all about that monster dorado, whose weight doesn't even matter because the fight it gave boiled down to some of the most spectacular fishing I'd ever experienced. To me, that fish was a thousand pounds of holy grail.

Not knowing much about dorado, but having heard that they change colors rapidly, I'd snapped some shots before it had gone into the hold just in case its spectrum faded. Strangely enough, when we came in twenty minutes later, the three smaller dorados had dulled a bit. But the big one, its gold was just as glimmery as when it had been in the sky going bonkers.

Even more ablaze than its colors, though, was what I realized later. That observation being: when we look at these truly bizarre, monstrous fish, we don't see vicious incarnations of nightmares as much as we see funny versions of our own muppet-selves.

But seriously folks, we do see ourselves when we look at these fish, and more than that, we see them from the point of view of a child. I mean, they're stripped down to their cartoon essentials: that comic mouth, those bubble eyes, the daffy shape of their doofy-looking heads with human expressions we can't help feeling connections with. Still, our

31. Monster dorado money shot. Photo by Lea Graham.

adult selves are capable of taking these associations further and making something of the reasons why we want to feel a kinship with animals that look like us. So let's get down to the nitty-gritty:

When we look at certain creatures, we see ourselves in Nature. And if we allow for the wiping out of creatures that look like us, this speaks volumes about how we can turn the other cheek. So when we see ourselves reflected in creatures, we see the roles we need to play in order to sustain ourselves—which brings me back to McGuane's thesis of putting back more than we take out.

Speaking on behalf of sportsmen and outdoorsy types (yep, I just elected myself), I say that because of the time we spend in the Wild, and because of what the Wild rewards us with, we have an intimate connection with Nature. And this intimacy, which stems from the knowledge that we've been blessed by the greatest of all possible outcomes, comes from knowing that Nature can save us from ourselves. That is, we recognize a healing faith in our chromosomes that we understand at a cellular level.

As my friend the eco-writer David Gessner states on his *Nat Geo Explorer* episode "Call of the Wild," "Science is proving what we've always known intuitively: nature does good things to the human brain. It makes us healthier, happier, and smarter." He goes on to say: "It turns out there's hard science behind this. . . . [Researchers] have proven that walking in nature reduces stress hormones and lowers blood pressure and heart rates . . . but they've also discovered something about trees that kind of blows my mind. Some trees like cypress give off chemical compounds called 'phytoncides.' We absorb the phytoncides and they promote our natural killer cells which help us fight cancer. We can experience a 40 percent increase in our natural killer cells from just walking in the woods."[10]

So if there's scientific evidence that being near trees can increase our chances of living longer and healthier, it's reasonable to make the logical leap that our proximity to water can do something similar. Because when it comes down to it, us outsidey folks know that being outside just makes us feel better, which has psychosomatic effects on our physiology. That's just all there is to it, and we know it in our DNA.

We also know that our relationship with the Wild is a privilege we must defend. This is our responsibility, or else we're irresponsible—especially when we know what Nature can do for us. That's why I call upon my own kind—anglers, hikers, canoers, mushroom hunters, and anyone else who just has to get out of town—to step it up with giving back.

But how do we do that? Well, we start by the taking time to sit down and have some serious conversations with ourselves. Then we set some goals so that when we look back on what we put back we'll see our reflections in the mirror and not feel like crap.

Those who partake of this challenge will differ in their approaches. Some might shoot to pick up litter, others might vow to revolutionize agricultural methods or discover the next alternative fuel. Some, however, have already been hard at work.

According to an article in *Fish2Fork* ("The campaigning restaurant guide for people who want to eat fish—sustainably"), leading fish distributers and supermarket conglomerates recently "called for immediate action to prevent overfished yellowfin tuna populations from collapsing within five years." Birdseye Foods, along with executives from thirty-seven other influential companies and the WWF, have petitioned the Indian Ocean Tuna Commission to reduce the harvesting of wild yellowfin by 20 percent to "ensure the sustainability of all Indian Ocean tuna stocks."[11]

Imagine that: CEOs actually fighting for balance in the ecosystem! Sure, their main impetus is to keep their businesses going, but here's what I'm looking at: if corporations can engage in meaningful activism, there's no reason why individuals can't do the same.

As for me, I'm going to make it my mission to come up with a more concrete idea about how I intend to put back more than I take out. Because at heart, putting back more is a matter of respect. It's a matter of respecting our place in the world, respecting other places in the world, and respecting ourselves. So in the interest of living up to this challenge, I'm imposing a deadline on myself: by the end of the next chapter. This will give me time to seriously reflect and have a productive dialogue with myself.

The conversation had begun.

9

Attack of the Italian Zander

Putting Back More Than We Take Out

THE ZANDER, OR PIKE PERCH, IS A EURASIAN COUSIN OF THE walleye that's been getting some negative publicity as being hostile to humans. There are numerous online videos of this fish allegedly attacking divers, but the most infamous incident harks back to 2009 when world headlines screamed versions of "Monster Fish Killed After Terrorising Swiss Swimmers." Reportedly, an eighteen-pound *Sander lucioperca* had gone amok in Switzerland's Lac Majeur. According to the United Kingdom's *Telegraph*, "Two swimmers were treated in hospital for bite wounds up to four inches long after being attacked at the lake, which borders Italy. . . . Police divers at first tried to capture the car-nivorous fish with a net, but when this failed, they pursued the zander with a harpoon and managed to kill it." The offending fish, which was suspected of "suffering from a hormonal imbalance," was then served up for dinner to placate tourists.[1]

This was an unusual event considering that zander are not known for fish-on-human violence. If anything, their reputation is that of a popular game fish prized for their delicate taste and flaky white flesh. As a food fish, they're farmed in aquaculture facilities like the AquaPri pike perch plant in Denmark. Perhaps that's where the Chippewa casino in Turtle Lake, Wisconsin, got its controversial zander fillets that it tried to pass off as walleye. Or even more ironic was the "Walleyegate" scandal of 2004 in which pike perch was substituted for walleye in some Twin Cities restaurants.

The reason I write "ironic" is because walleye is the official Minnesota state fish, and with Minneapolis being my home town, and me being an obsessive fisherman, you'd think I'd have more of a relationship with "walleyed pike." But I never caught very much of that fish or even had much of an awareness of it. For me, they were always a bycatch, so it's ironic to me that a half-century-old Minnesota fisherman would take an interest in the *Percidae* family. Especially after moving to Arkansas, which for decades boasted a world record, nonnative twenty-two-pounder.

Zander don't get much bigger than that. Under unusual conditions, they're supposedly capable of reaching four feet.[2] The current IGFA world record is a twenty-five-pounder from Switzerland. Pictured here is a monster-sized zander in that same weight class caught in Italy by Dino Ferrari, the "bro" who caught that wels catfish that weighed almost three hundred pounds. The weight of his zander, however, went unrecorded.

Hence, with the knowledge that there are monster zanders out there, and with accusations of thug behavior, this was a species I had to investigate as a potential monster fish. And since I was in Florence on a research-based leave of absence, and since I had the opportunity to do some fact-finding in Italy, I took it.

On my way to meet fishing guide Oliver Howard for some zandering, I had time to sit down in a park and break out my notebook. It was time to have that serious conversation with myself about how I could put back more than I take out, and I was dreading the confrontation. Because what if I couldn't live up to the challenge I had issued to others and myself? Or what if I was on the wrong track? Like maybe I should be thinking more about tackle or tactics rather than focusing on my own eco-centric indulgences. Whatever the case, I started jotting:

1. Teach more environmental courses because that's the most important thing I do on this planet

32. Monster zander. Courtesy of Dino Ferrari.

2. Shoot to publish eco-essays in magazines and journals that communicate with a wider audience

3. Ask myself this question every year (how to put back more?)

4. Take kids fishing

5. Ask others this question every year (how to put back more?)

6. Do more community water quality work, which I've been slacking on

7. Take a bag to pick up litter whenever I go hiking

8. Put litter in my boat when I go fishing

9. Take adults fishing

10. Don't look for a silver bullet, but look instead for myriad ways to help an ecosystem out

11. Look for myriad ecosystems to help out

12. Consider running for public office on the Green Party ticket—not now, but after retirement

13. Actually research what I can do for the environment

14. Volunteer for environmentally related activities (brainstorm more on this later)
15. Live healthier so as to live longer so as to give back more
16. Consider running for public office as a Democrat (or as a Republican??)
17. Write annual letters to the editor regarding environmental concerns
18. Buy land to protect (make sure there's good fishing there)
19. Revise #3; make this list an ongoing project and add to it whenever a thought hits me
20. Revise #5; ask others this question more frequently than annually— not just to get more ideas for myself, but to get others thinking about this too

Voila! I suddenly had twenty ideas in twenty minutes, and starting the dialogue wasn't as hard as I thought it would be.

The fishing, on the other hand, would prove to be more challenging.

I met Ollie on the Ponte alle Grazie. His guide service, Fishing in Florence, specialized in connecting clients with *siluro* (wels catfish), carp, and other species in the Arno River. I'd met Ollie the other day for a strategizing beer and liked him right off the bat. A young Brit who'd graduated from Oxford University, he was a fellow English major who had decided to concentrate on his passion for birds and fish. In the process, he'd done some conservation work setting up nesting boxes throughout Florence and had written a book about birds in the region. He'd also established himself as an extremely successful and ambitious guide. What I really appreciated, though, was the way he looked at the river as an artery rich in biodiversity cutting through the middle of the city.

Anyway, we were shooting to fish for zander at night, and since it was only two in the afternoon, we had a few hours before sunset. So we went downstream to a pool where a 260-pound siluro was trapped, and he rigged me up with a heavy-duty casting rod and some modified

Rapala lures. I put on a pair of waders, Ollie instructed me on the proper depth and speed for the lure, and I got out in the water.

It was an impressive spot and cool to know that just upstream Michelangelo's *David* continued to endure as a mind-blowing masterpiece. Botticelli's overrated *Birth of Venus* was there as well, in the company of some extremely expressive Leonardos in the Uffizi, all within spitting distance of the Baroquely ornate yet Gothic Duomo, which is symbolic of this cultural center for art and aesthetics in Italy.

"Aesthetics," of course, meaning what people look for in beauty, a word I explain to my poetry students as something that has different connotations for different individuals. The example I always provide is that of a big old ugly catfish, which might not look beautiful to them, but when I see one, I see an epitome of beauty. Which is why I was fishing on the Arno right now.

Meanwhile, Ollie had set up a lighter-weight rod and was searching the shores for signs of zander. But something wasn't right about the water. The color was off due to a recent rain. The river was also running a bit fast and high.

Then, when the sun went down, Ollie told me he wasn't feeling very optimistic about getting zander. He recommended going out for a beer and trying at a later date, which sounded good to me.

So that's what we did, followed by another beer. We talked about fish, showed each other some cell phone photos, and discussed some human beings as well. I was sincerely interested in his work, and the feeling was mutual. By the time we said "ciao," we had made a connection, and I was looking forward to going out again when the conditions were more optimal.

I met my next guide, Fabrizio Terenghi, in the city of Como in northern Italy, just south of the Swiss border. He picked me up at the Best Western Continental, and by 5:45 p.m. we were in the city center on Lake Como, surrounded by towering monuments and griffins carved in stone. It was dark out, and foggy clouds were concealing the dramatic mountains descending almost vertically into the lake, but I could feel them all around us. I could also feel the steady drizzle.

Fabrizio handed me a superlight spinning rod with a gunmetal-gray rubber jig on it and took a heavier rod with a crankbait for himself. We went to the concrete wall and started casting. Nothing. Nothing but the awesome mountains I couldn't see with homes lit up like Christmas trees, including George Clooney's mansion.

After a bit, we moved to a spot along a manicured parkway that could've been in Paris or Vienna or New York City. There was a sand beach beneath the wall we were casting from, and an injured mallard was getting battered by the waves. I don't know what his deal was, but I couldn't help not being concerned.

A half hour later, we moved on to the harbor. We were on a walkway cutting across the cove and there were dog walkers and lovers strolling arm in arm. It started raining a bit harder, and I felt my fingers getting numb. Nevertheless, I kept up a steady rhythm of casting, letting the jig sink to the bottom, giving it a couple cranks, then letting it sink again to simulate an injured minnow.

Then one hit, just like that, and I reeled in my target fish. It was a little zander, just ten inches long, torpedo-shaped and healthy. It looked like a whittled-down walleye built for speed. Wow! I'd gotten what I'd come to get.

"You got the little one," Fabrizio said as I tossed it back. "Next you will get the medium one."

I kept on casting in the same spot. There was a lot of activity there with fish breaking the surface alongside the boats. Fabrizio suspected they were perch. I figured something was either feeding there or forcing up smaller fish. I also figured that zander must have excellent vision to be feeding at night.

Then, wham! I got another, and this one was bigger. It started giving my lightweight rod the business, but I brought it in, white belly gleaming in the rain. It was the medium-sized zander Fabrizio had predicted, and since it was too heavy to reel in, he lifted it in by the line and laid it down on the planks, a sturdy sixteen-incher somewhere between two and three pounds. Victory again!

33. The zander that didn't get away. Photo by Fabrizio Terenghi.

I could see the pikey quality of this species even more than in the fish before. This pike perch was way more missile-like than a walleye in both shape and attitude. It seemed to me that with their fancy, fanning dorsal fins, walleye are more elegant, and that the zander model is stealthier. Whatever the case, it was a badass-looking fish.

Both of us kept casting. I was really feeling it, and after a bit, I brought in another fish. This one was a *cavedano*, or European chub, probably pushing five pounds. Fabrizio was amazed by its size. Like the other fish, we let it go.

Then I got another fish.

"You are magic, my friend," Fabrizio said, trying to unsnag his line. He'd lost a few lures and had been tangled up a few times, but since I was getting the fish, it was a successful night for both of us.

This one was a "real perch," as Fabrizio called it. It looked like a yellow perch but was gray in coloration.

"Bye bye, guy," I told it, and let it go.

It wasn't even nine o'clock, and we still had two hours to go, but I was satisfied enough to pack up early. I was hankering for a beer and hungry for dinner, and besides, I was wet to the shivering point. But most of all, since I'd caught what I'd come to get, this meant that we could concentrate on a different monster fish in the morning, one that was a longtime favorite for both of us: pike!

We arrived at Lago di Pusiano on the outskirts of Como at seven in the morning. Cicco (pronounced "Cheecho") was readying the boat, which was powered by an electric trolling motor because no gas motors were allowed on the lake except for law enforcement. Fabrizio had referred to Cicco as "The Zander Master" and had told me about the twenty-two-pounder he'd caught, which was the second-largest known zander ever caught in Italy.

Out on the lake, the fog was just beginning to lift. There was a fish called *scardola* breaking the surface everywhere, and two huge swans immediately came over majestically begging for some bread. But there were also plenty of diving birds, ducks, gulls, mud hens, crows, and herons in the area.

As the fog began to lift off the lake, I saw that we were once again in a dramatic alpine basin. Mountains rose insanely steeply all around us in the burnt umber of fall turning gold. There was an ambery luminescence to everything that was casting the greenery in a vibrant apricot light. Idyllic rooftops and steeples were poking up from the lush as they have for centuries.

Fabrizio rigged me up with an eight-inch chubster of a white rubber worm that swam like a fish, and my guides began alternating between similar lures and some smaller jigs that looked like frizzy pink tutus. We fished some brush piles, got no action whatsoever, then went out to an island owned by an eccentric banker. We saw three wallabies roaming free, and there were African storks and obsidian peacocks strutting the shoreline. We fished there for an hour, but again, nothing.

That's when Cicco decided to make things happen, or so he joked as he took a leak into a plastic container then dumped the contents overboard. "You'll see," he told us in Italian.

We moved over to some tall, wickery grass, worked the shore for ten minutes, and then something hit my line. It was a blazing green and yellow bass that dropped jaws as we netted it: a four-pound largemouth that they couldn't stop whistling at. Apparently, they don't get much larger than that in these here parts.

What I wanted, though, was a mongo pike, so we got back to casting, Cicco claiming that his "magic pee" had attracted the bass. We laughed at that, and I made a joke about how I should bottle some and take some back to the United States, to which Fabrizio replied that I might have some trouble at the airport.

That's when a monster pike appeared. It followed Cicco's lure in, and we saw it hovering thick and green right beneath us, almost a meter long, before sinking into the algae-colored depths.

"Drop, drop!" Fabrizio exclaimed, motioning for me to open my bale so my lure could follow it down. We all did that, jigging and casting in the vicinity, but the fish was clearly spooked.

The morning went on, sometimes raining lightly, sometimes not. It was pretty cold and damp, but we all had rain jackets and warm clothes. Then Fabrizio's pole bent into an arc.

Knees bent to absorb the shock (a technique I'd never seen before), he eventually horsed it over to the boat. It was a solid pike. In fact, it was the same pike we'd seen before. Both Fabrizio and Cicco recognized it, and after a lot of resistance they finally got it into the net.

We were now totally stoked, slapping palms and taking pictures. The beast must've weighed fifteen pounds. It was greenish blue and covered with a white ovally pattern on the sides with bubbles of froth all over it. Like the bass, it was catch and release.

Again, Fabrizio and I bowed down to Cicco's magic pee, which he claimed had a duration of three to four hours. Cicco then made a joke having to do with what the results would be if he were to upgrade his contribution to the lake—a suggestion Fabrizio emphatically discouraged.

It was time for lunch, so we pulled up to the municipal dock. There was a five-foot-long dead siluro on the shore with a patch of flesh nibbled off its tail by some small animal. There was also a live siluro of the same size strung to the dock. I went over and checked it out. It had that black-and-gold speckilization I'd seen on a wels I'd caught in Spain, and it splashed all over when I hefted it up to snap a few pictures. Must've weighed eighty pounds.

Fabrizio talked to the fishery guys and purchased my license, then told me they were keeping those cats for a scientist who was coming to take some tissue samples. I didn't get much more info than that, but if they were testing fish for anything, that's progressive. Just like the city's solar-powered sight-seeing boat anchored near the dock.

Reflecting on this, I couldn't help adding "Go solar" to my list of what I could give back. Going solar, however, is a lot easier to think about than do, and it can be expensive in the short term. But it's something to think about, especially if you can pay it forward to the grid. That's what we need to be moving toward, the idea of every building being its own power source.

Anyhow, we warmed up, ate some paninis, then got back out there. It was still raining on and off, and the windchill was pretty harsh, but we continued to tough it out. After another hour, Fabrizio added his own magic pee to the lake, and then I made a donation of my own.

Minutes later, Cicco the Zander Master hooked up with a fish. He brought it in from the stern, and its massive gray tones and flaring gills gave it away. It was a monster zander, well over two feet long. I netted it, and again there was jubilation.

My magic pee was credited for attracting this fish as we shot some pictures, then let it go. All of us had now caught a good fish, and because these were basically the fish I'd grown up with, the whole experience was rewarding in a nostalgic way. Still, I was longing for my own pike, which would really make for a feeling of completion.

When it hit an hour later, I thought it was a tree stump. I yanked back, and it didn't budge. Fabrizio advised me to ease it up. I did, and it was like hoisting a waterlogged limb from the muck. Then I felt that familiar shimmy of a muscly fish powering down. It gave a nice run, taking out ten yards of line. Then I brought it back again. It went right into the net, and suddenly I had my pike. It was probably a dozen pounds.

This was one of those fishing trips when everything had gone according to plan. That is, we all got the fish we wanted, and we were all charged with the type of exhilarating exhaustion an angler fishes all day to get. The next stop, therefore, would be the bar.

Later, looking at Cicco's zander on my phone, the thing that struck me the most was the teeth. They were right there at the end of its dagger-toothed head on its steely, streamlined body: four sharp-as-hell, flesh-rending superfangs, two pointing up, two pointing down. Not only that, they were curving backward to prevent prey from slipping away. They were wicked-looking teeth, lethal-looking teeth, teeth that made the zander vicious in appearance. Man, those teeth were the teeth of nightmares. And because they were designed for snapping down and hanging on, they instantly explained to me why those Swiss swimmers had been "terrorised."

Not only that, but zander teeth have an actual history of inflicting harm on actual humans, which has resulted in stitches for an actual

34. Spitzer bags a pike. Photo by Fabrizio Terenghi.

reason—one that sent me straight to YouTube to further research zander attacks. The foremost video was titled "Aggressive Zander Attacks Divers."[3] Still, it only nipped a single diver, and that's after he provoked it. As any viewer can see, that zander is already suffering from an injury above its eye. There's a loose flap of skin there, most likely due to the fighting that comes with competition for spawning. That zander was standing its ground, refusing to leave, so there was definitely something altruistic keeping it there.

Let's not beat around the bush anymore. The "actual reason" I mention above is obvious, which is why I can't help agreeing with the responses posted in the comments section following that video. Big Dog writes, "The title is wrong . . . the Zander is not aggressive. . . . More like annoyed Zander defends against annoying divers." HoppyFishPerse001 echoes this sentiment with, "You guys should respect him [rather] than harassing. Zander has risen his fins to warn you guys but he knows he cant do much. Kinda feel bad for the fish." GPC adds, "Two bullies harassing a *Sander lucioperca* that is protecting his eggs." Ed Dost then puts it all in perspective as a "zander protecting its offspring, should have left it alone."

As another YouTube video, "Zander on the Nest Attacks Three Times," demonstrates, this species doesn't differentiate between humans and inanimate objects; they're just programmed to try to scare off any threat to their DNA. In this video, a zander bites an irritating rubber lure that it's clearly not interested in eating because it spits it out thrice—as would any fish guarding its young.[4] Just like the zander in "Klopeiner See Zander Attacks Diver," and all the other videos of zander harassment I could find.[5]

That's what happened in Switzerland when that zander was hunted and harpooned to death for the most parental of actions any species could ever take next to procreation. It's the same story as that demonized wels in Berlin's Lake Waidsee, or any sunfish that ever nipped any bather on any gravel bar in the summer. It's just ridiculous to persecute any creature for guarding its young—as if we have more right to be in its environment than it does. I mean, get real, people! Do fish come to your home and menace your kids, antagonize you, then serve you up for dinner?

Hell no! But clearly, media outlets like the *Telegraph* implicate fish as "hormonally imbalanced" to reframe natural behaviors as crimes against humanity. But I wouldn't call that "monstrous;" I'd just call it misleading, as well as indicative of an adolescent mentality that's swift to accuse women of behaving emotionally due to egg generation.

Which leads to another thing the *Telegraph* got wrong: in the case of zander, the nests are guarded by the males.

Back in Florence a few days later I found myself with Ollie on the Arno, zandering again. I also found the narrative taking an unexpected turn. Rather than conveniently winding up by focusing on my target fish, I'd returned to the question of how to put back.

Both the water and air were damn cold, and I wasn't feeling very hopeful of catching anything that morning. Casting a floating Rapala, I'd come to the point where I knew I was a hypocrite. Not in what I say or write, but in how I live. Whereas Lea and I were spending the semester together, we usually don't get that luxury. When we're in the

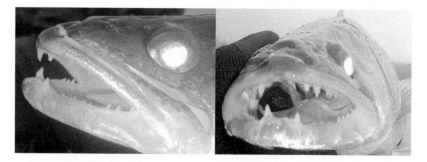

35. Monster zander teeth designed for biting the crap out of anything that threatens their young. Photos by Mark Spitzer.

states, we fly across the country every few weeks, leaving vapor trails that translate to at least 2,200 round-trip miles every time we visit each other. That's why I went to carbonfootprint.com to estimate how much CO_2 I purchase and pump into the atmosphere every time I make that trip.[6] It came out to be .29 metric tons, which is 639 pounds of planet-warming molecules floating around in the sky thanks to me. But that's not the price I pay for love; that's the price the environment pays.

I could go in several directions from here. I could try to justify my actions as an eco-writer who pollutes, or I could make a case for being a victim of a system that doesn't give us much choice. The fact of the matter, though, is that a gallon of gas weighs 6.18 pounds, and according to the U.S. Energy Administration, when we burn a gallon of that heroin it puts an average of 19.6 pounds of carbon dioxide into the sky.[7] Diesel adds a couple pounds more, and biodiesel is a couple pounds less, but what I don't understand is how it's possible for something to increase three times in mass.

So I sent an email to my buddy Turkey Buzzard. He's a chemistry professor, and he performed some calculations that came up with a similar figure. He replied that "in extracting fossil fuel, then refining it, then burning it, we're definitely changing the chemistry of the air, and that is the key issue."[8]

In the meantime, our freedom to pollute is lending to a sea level rise of "between 7 and 23 inches . . . by century's end." That stat comes from

National Geographic News, who estimate that a million species will be extinct in three decades.[9]

My fingers were now numb from exposure, but I kept on casting anyway and thinking more bummer thoughts. Like how my demand for what I want supplied in my life is destroying what I love the most: the space this planet provides for us to live and die with animals, including each other. Because here I am, adding to that annihilation—which is what makes this question so personally urgent for me. Because if you know you're responsible, and if you don't try to reverse the damage you've done, then you're just as much part of the problem as those who actively seek to profit off ignorance.

If anything, that's the monster we're facing now. It took billions of years to get to this flash of livable oxygen levels that are only sustainable for an instant in which a delicate balance of acids and carbon and water and heat is being taken for granted. An instant in which I don't see any god with any magic wand or will to quick-fix what we have irreversibly shot to hell. And even if we could convert to "cleaner fuels" right now and increase education yesterday, we'd only be sustaining a planet on life support. That's just a fact, and our fisheries are the measure of that. They measure the health of our water, our air, our entire biosphere. Time has run out. There is no magic pee.

Dwelling on such dark thoughts, this would've been a good time to have hooked a zander. But that just wasn't in the cards. Sometimes you catch 'em, sometimes you don't, and sometimes celebrating a victory just isn't appropriate considering what's at stake.

So when the end of the day came around, and I still hadn't caught a zander, I wasn't disappointed. Because really, I'd already gotten what I needed, including a sobering dose of owning my own guilt. But what can you do with that?

Winter had set in.

Then it got even colder. Especially on that gray rainy day when the Divided States of America (with a little help from Russia) elected a climate change denier for president who the Center for Biodiversity has characterized as an "unprecedented threat to our nation's democracy, health, wildlife and environment," and who threatens "to dismantle the Environmental Protection Agency, gut the Clean Air Act and Endangered Species Act . . . [and] eliminate regulations protecting poor communities from pollution."[10] That's when I, like millions of others, found myself in tears for what I feared would happen to your world and my world and our world as we know it. That's when I had to be completely honest with myself and actually accept my guilt rather than just feel it. And that's when I didn't just think it—I knew it for sure: we all take out more than we can possibly put back. That's just the way it is.

Thus, to ward off the toxic cloud rolling over everything, I had to answer my own pressing question of how to give back more than I take out. Otherwise, I'd just keep blithering like a powerless little weakling. So to placate myself and nobody else, this is what I came up with.

Back when I was a graduate student at the University of Colorado, a professor gave me some game-changing advice. I was young and idealistic and excited by studying creative writing and imagining where it would lead. That professor was the poet Lorna Dee Cervantes, and the class was eco-poetics, a subject that inspired me to write like a maniac whose motto was "quantity over quality." That's how I trained myself to pump it out every day. Nobody needed to tell me to take notes or do my research. Nobody had to assign me a minimum page count. I was on fire. I was a machine. And when I went to conference with Lorna, I was surprised to hear her tell me, "Whatever you're doing, it's working, so just keep doing it."

One question Lorna put to students in that class was the question of "What's important?" I won't even get into how that question affected us, but I can say that in considering it, divorces happened, some dropped out, some came out, and others went absolutely looney tunes. But this question made us realize what we needed to fight for and how we needed to do it. Still, a quarter century later, it's a question I ask myself every single day.

What I realize now is that if we want to give back as much as we can for what's most important, then we can't settle for a single definitive answer when we need to operate on multiple fronts. Essentially, we are like sharks that rely on ram ventilation for filtering oxygen. If they stop moving, they drown. Likewise, if we stop trying to answer our most important questions, we fail to grow as a species.

In other words, the question of giving back has become my elusive stingray. And that's what it needs to be, always out there swimming around, leading me to other fish.

And that's my panacea as well: don't answer the damn question; just keep on asking it and doing as much as I can in ways that have proven effective in the past. Meaning doing this! Exactly this! For what's important! Because this is the most I can do.

That's what I caught from going after zander, and it's good enough for me.

And because of that, the question then reverses itself.

It looks you in the eye. It asks you what your own answer is.

And then, just to be an ass, it asks you if your answer is good enough for you.

10

Translating an Eely Ionian Monsterfest into Top Predator Decimation

More Than Just a Metaphor

THE SIZE OF CONGER EELS HAS BEEN GREATLY EXAGGERATED. In 2015, a 130-pounder was caught off the southwest coast of England, and it didn't take long for its two meters in length to triple in size. The word got out that a twenty-foot monster eel had been hauled from the depths of the Atlantic, due in part to a photo that plays with perspective. According to the United Kingdom's *Daily Mail Online*, a fisherman later admitted to the hoax.[1]

Despite such egregious rumors, the European conger eel (*Conger conger*) is the largest member of the eel family and is capable of reaching lengths of ten feet. Meanwhile, there are no shortages of credible internet photos of guys posing with congers of jaw-dropping proportions. When I first stumbled upon images of six- and seven-footers, I was blown away by how goliath this true sea serpent is, and how the bigger it gets, the fuglier it gets.

But what amazed me even more were the untapped possibilities of this fish. First, they are definitely fierce enough to qualify as monster fish. Secondly, considering the global range of this fish family, we really don't have much of an awareness of them. In fact, they've only been featured on a handful of TV shows. Even Jeremy Wade has yet to investigate the brutal crimes of this behemoth.

36. The mythical beast. Courtesy of Apex News and Pictures.

Hence, I was attracted to the idea of studying the conger eel for the same reason that I used to translate "lost" texts by French criminals and sociopaths. Sure, I'd seen opportunities to publish "secondary" or "minor" works, but more than that, I'd been interested in researching literature with a bastard status in order to bring overlooked writings that were well worth experiencing into the light.

So with a similar mission in mind, I lit off to the Ionian Sea at the bottom of the inner bootheel of Italy to translate the *il grongo* experience. And, I should add, it was the place to go because up in Tuscany, December was cold and sucky, and down in the South, it was warm and sunny and the congers were reportedly biting.

Lea came along, and we were struck by the brilliant, transparent cerulean of the sea. Strolling along the Roman-era walkways and medieval ramparts of Gallipoli, we could see schools of fish crossing the rubble of centuries as old men repaired nets.

The first place we went was the Al Pescatore Hotel to drop off our backpacks, and the next place we went was the seafood market down at the port. Within minutes, I saw my first conger eels along with fresh-caught oysters, clams, crabs, monkfish, and more. Those eels, though, were pretty small, and could hardly be thought of as monsters at all. They weren't much longer than two feet, each with a slit behind the head. I'd seen a TV show in which a fisherman recommended severing the spine in that spot as the quickest, most efficient way to dispatch of a conger eel, so it doesn't slither and snap all over the boat and bite someone's finger off.

But there were also immature tuna being sold, which seems to be the universal story for this fish. I took a picture of one, thereby adding another JPEG to my ongoing archive of juvenile tuna being harvested worldwide.

Anyway, it was lunch time, so we stopped at La Lampara Pescheria and ordered some white wine. The owner gave us two raw shrimps, which we ate sashimi-style as was the local custom. Then four oysters arrived with lemons to squeeze over them and were predictably magnificent. The vongole clams, however, were exquisite. Their bloodred meat was swimming in a wine-like sauce which we slurped off the half shell in frontal-lobe-exploding ecstasy. This was followed by an octopus grilled just enough to make it not raw, the perfect plushness of its flesh slathered in rosemarried olive oil sprinkled with sea salt. Three king prawns then added some interactive digit-licking to what, I decided, was the Ultimate Seafood Splendor of our seafood-seeking existence together.

And dinner that night was equally as *perfetto*. We ate at a place called Portolano, run by Franco and Lucia, who welcomed us with a flourish of savory squid fritters. Those juicy gems of just the right chewiness were complemented by a lightly fried cod and cabbage dish, goldenly crusted anchovies with their heads on, a creamy combination of mashed potatoes and buttery fish in which you couldn't tell where one stopped and the other began, a sweet and sour eggplant dish that electrified the taste buds, a wet dream of an octopus pasta in a spicy orange picante, homemade bread baked with rich black olives inside, and marinated artichoke hearts—and that was just the *apertivo*. When the main courses arrived, we could only eat a few bites. Still, we finished our bottle of wine, plus some grappa and a macchiato, not to mention a slice of cake.

Point being: we had hit pay dirt paradise, which was exactly what we needed since our time in Italy was coming to an end, and soon we'd be heading back to the uncertainty of postelection America.

That evening, the seas had been too rough to go out on, so my guide Luca De Prezzi gave me a choice. Leave at 3:00 a.m. the first night, or at 3:00 a.m. the second night. I wasn't thrilled by either of these choices, but since we'd traveled ten hours to get there, and since I might never get a chance to go eeling on the Ionian again, I chose the first night. That way I'd have a day to recover and hang out before we had to travel.

When the alarm rang at quarter to three, I dragged my groggy butt out of bed, put on all the layers of clothing I had (including two pairs of pants), and stumbled down to the port bar. I'd gotten three and a half hours of sleep thanks to the wine, the grappa, and a self-induced food coma, so I slugged down a regrettable Red Bull and waited for Luca to arrive.

He pulled up, and we shot off to a café where we downed an espresso, filled a thermos full of more, and met Antonio. Neither of them spoke English, and I sure as *merda* couldn't speak a lick of Italiano. We communicated mostly through sporadic gestures and Google Translate on an iPad.

Fifteen minutes later, we were motoring out of the harbor under the brisk black sky in a twenty-foot open boat with an inboard motor and tiller. En route, we stopped by another boat, and Luca placed a baitfish on an outboard engine. He told me that he was playing a prank on a friend.

It took about forty-five minutes to get to the spot where we began laying the longline, which was a method I was eager to try. In a sense, a longline is an extra-extra-extra-long trotline, which is one of my preferred techniques in Arkansas. You never know what you're going to catch, and when you go to the trouble of placing a whole lot of hooks in the water, you can catch the hell out of them.

Antonio dropped in the first anchor, which was attached to a float and more than two miles of hundred-pound monofilament. Yep, that's right: two miles! And every twenty feet, there was a four- to eight-foot dropline of lighter test attached, each of those baited with a bloody chunk of anchovy. It was all arranged in a tub the size of a semi tire, the bait hanging on the outer edge.

Luca piloted the craft, puttering slowly through the dark, and Antonio unwound as we went. His arms were working at an inhuman speed, flashing like propellers you couldn't see. I was so impressed that I shot a video, marveling at how he dealt with tangles and loops, twirling the bait over the main line with astonishing dexterity. He was working like a professional who'd been doing this all his life—just like his father, no doubt, and his father's father, and generations of fathers before him.

Of course, I worried that he might get snagged because that's what happens all over the world with this type of fishing. Everywhere and every year, sleepy or sloppy fishermen get hooked, pulled in, and drowned by big fish or machinery.

But there was another hazard I was aware of: a boat coming along and severing the longline. After an hour of laying it down, that would totally blow. Losing tackle is never any fun.

Whatever the case, we finally got to the end and dropped in the other anchor and float. The longline settled on the bottom where it could avoid the chop of a prop, so now it was time to do some squidding. Luca broke out two handlines with crankbaits that looked like standard minnow lures, but instead of trailing treble hooks, there were forward-pointing spikes at the tips of the tails which could impale a squishy squid like a frog gig in a cow pie. We then tooled around with the lures trolling behind us for over an hour, swinging our wrists to make them rise and dive. But in the end, no attack of the squid took place.

Fingers numb from the cold, but stomachs warmed by espresso, we returned to the first float at around six in the morning and got in position. I was up front hauling in the main line as the droplines slid toward Antonio. If there was bait on the hook, he'd perform a spinning motion, smack it on the hull, and the meat would burst apart. The entire longline went into the tub—droplines, hooks, everything—with no arranging. But once in a while, we'd snag some seaweed. When this happened, it was pretty easy to just pop the line and lose the hook.

Then we got a major snag, so Luca put it in neutral. Antonio asked for an iron ring. It was the size of a car steering wheel and had been cut clean through in one spot where a rubber sleeve covered the gap. Antonio slipped the main line through the gap, reapplied the sleeve, then let the ring, which was attached to a rope, follow the main line down to the bottom. Then he did a bunch of maneuvers, lifting and pulling the ring around under water. It was a tedious process, but one that had been perfected through the centuries, and it was effective in getting longlines back. If he hadn't been able to get that line back, we would've had to have gone to the other end and started from the other direction with the probability of getting snagged again.

We moved along gradually, and eventually something coppery began flashing below us. It was a moray eel twisting around itself. Antonio pulled it in and Luca cut the line. He threw it in a bucket, and we continued on. Empty hook after empty hook we continued on. Then we caught a small octopus all lit up by the high-powered onboard lamp. Then more nothing.

The sun was coming up when we hit the next major snag. Antonio worked on it for fifteen minutes, which disgruntled them but not me. The more our lines were in the water, I figured, the better our chances would be of getting a conger eel.

Basically, I was betting on this fish to provide the final chapter. If I got skunked, I'd have to go back to teaching and it might be a year before I'd be able to finish my monster-fish book. More importantly, due to recent political developments, I felt the need to add to a dialogue that was now way more urgent than it had ever been before.

Anyway, Antonio finally hoisted the problem to the surface. It was a huge commercial fishing net. He then pulled it out of the water, and Luca passed the longline tub under the mesh. Apparently, a fishing boat had come along while we were out squidding and had laid its net over our line—an annoyance of the trade which happens all too much.

And as dawn dawned, I saw four large buoys running along the shore we were paralleling. Out in the sea a mile away, there were four commercial fishing boats with seine nets attached to those buoys. Consequently, we had to go through the process four more times, which my guides did good-naturedly.

Then, during the untangling of the last net, my bladder caught up with me, so I took a leak into the sea. This would be the test, I chuckled to myself, to see if magic pee applied to salt water.

Now I'm not saying that *you're in* for good luck when *you're in* a boat *urinating*, but after that, we really started hooking fish. We got another moray eel, then a tiny rockfish, then a solid silvery fish with a tough-looking jaw, then more morays, but no conger eels. Man, we caught starfish and more octopi; a strange, little, pugnacious fellow; a burly, bassy-looking fish; and something that a waiter in Trieste had called "Luigi." We probably caught a dozen moray eels, and when they were longer than two feet, Luca would brain them with a steel pipe.

Then, toward the end of the longline, something white and snaky

37. Conger eel monster fish! Photo by Luca De Prezzi.

began whirling up. But it was only white because of the light bouncing off its skin.

"Conger! Conger!" Antonio sang, and I netted it. It was three feet long and going nuts.

Two more *grongos* followed, one of them over a meter long. We put them in a cooler filled with seawater, and I was buzzing at that slaphappy level where lack of sleep synergizes with great elation and absolutely nothing can bring you down.

Since the previous chapter involved some grave reflection, I knew that scoring these congers would steer the book in a much more positive direction, which is the tone I wanted the journey to end on. But more than that, that's what happened. Not only did I get my monster fish, I got a whole boatful of them.

Let's start with the conger eels, which, if they didn't have such vicious associations and mythical histories as part of their context, I'd say were beautiful. No—I *do* say they're beautiful! The three we caught were sleek and streamlined and soft. Their heads were shapely, their eyes were comely, and they even had pleasant expressions with long, happy grins.

The morays were definitely much more grotesque and incendiary to the eye. They had this super-crazy paisley pattern of electric saffron blazing against a slick-skinned canvas of deep, purply browns—colors I couldn't really pin down because they just kept swirling psychedelically. And their heads: Jesus, their heads! You could see the power in their jaws, which resembled vise grips. And when those jaws were gaping, you could see their gleaming scimitar teeth. Their nostrils even had these nozzly, flaring flaps that looked like barbels and added an intimidating dragon factor. And at the point where their heads connected with their necks, they just sorta hunchbacked out all shouldery and muscly like weight-lifting bullies on steroids.

Plus, those eels were mean as hell. There was a moment when I was reaching into a bucket to poke a small fish, and one of the morays lurched like lightning for my wrist, trying to get me. I retracted in the nick of time, but Luca warned me with a firm "Attento!" When I looked at the

38. Moray monster fish! Photo by Mark Spitzer.

hand he was holding up, I saw one finger bent at a disturbing angle. I don't know if he was showing me that finger or raising all five to stress caution, but the bone had unquestionably been broken and reset off kilter.

Later on, peering into that bucket again, I saw one of the morays clamped on to the gut of another. Those eels were writhing and fighting, so I can see where they get their reputation for unruly violence. A few species are even venomous, and when they latch on to a human hand, their hook-shaped rear teeth don't release, so they have to be pried off.

Then there were the other bycatches, like our bluefish. With that belligerent lower jaw, angry eyes, and silver-bullet-body, this fierce, strong cannibal has been known to take chomps out of folks.

The goldblotch grouper was also an impressive made-for-battle-looking fish. Its massive maw of skewery was designed to engulf prey and pin victims like a bear trap. The IGFA record is barely three pounds, but if you're a crustacean, it'll kick your puny ass.

But sometimes the smallest monsters are the scariest because they pack the largest punch. Like the weever we caught, which derives its name from the Old French word "wivre," which comes from the Latin "vipera," meaning serpent. With its pugilistic lower jaw and blunt head

tapering toward its tail, its serrated fins and serpentine form are sug-
gestive of a medieval dagger. It even has a switchblade dorsal tucked in
its nape which unfortunate swimmers have been stung with. The pain
burns worse than stepping on a hornets' nest and can lead to headaches,
nausea, burning urination, tremors, severe heart rhythms, breathing
problems, seizures, gangrene, tissue degeneration, and unconsciousness.
No wonder Luca had snipped that spike immediately.

Then there were the octopi.

Luca broke out two huge handlines wound with what looked like
two-hundred-pound mono. At the end of each line was a one-pound
weight shaped like a pylon. Above that, the last sixteen inches of each
line held multiple colorful lures, silver spinners the size of shoehorns,
eel tails, decapitated baitfish, what looked like homemade ghosts made
from red and white plastic bags, and a chicken foot.

"Bawk bawk," Antonio clucked, and chucked them over the stern.

We then chugged around dragging the bottom with what looked like
the stuff attached to a "Just Married" car bumper. We employed a swinging motion as we did when we fished for squid. The octopi see all this junk
bouncing along on the sand and just can't help rushing over to grapple it.

Antonio caught the first one, and brought it in swiftly so it wouldn't let
go. He dropped it on the deck and it raced around at Mach speed with
all those whacko tentacles pulling its plasticity back and forth, its entire
weird body frantically reshaping itself as it shot out a swirl of black ink.

The second one he caught was the biggest, maybe two feet from the
tip of arm #1 to the end of arm #8. It wasn't monstrously enormous,
but it was still pretty alien in shape and form, especially with those
bulbous human eyes telepathically shooting the question straight into
my brain of whether it's ethical to eat a lifeform that could very well be
the evolution we're heading for.

I caught the third, and when I held it up for a photo, it was like
holding on to a shape-shifting slime creature from outer space. Gen-
Xers will remember that green substance called Slime that came in a
toy trashcan and how it oozed between your fingers when you tried to
grip it. That's what it's like trying to hold an octopus, except that it was

39. Antonio (*left*) and Spitzer (*right*) with mini
monstro octo. Photo by Luca De Prezzi.

also scrambling all over my wrist and sucking on with suction cups. I
was trying to keep its oyster-shattering beak away from my fingers, and
every cell in my body was wiggling with wariness of this mollusk of a
cephalopod that is so unlike us and so like us at the same time that it
curdles the plasma to hold one in your hand.

So there I had it: another addition to an unforeseen monsterfest that
continued to inject sizzling adrenal catalysts through all my molecular
tubeways. Because what can excite your inner kid more than meeting
freaky creatures? If you ask me, not much!

Though I'd originally come for the conger, I'd gravitated toward the
moray, at least in my interest in eating an eel. The morays just looked

so much more horrific than the congers that I had to try one. Also, they were more plentiful than the congers, so I could live with that.

When I approached the desk clerk at the Fisherman's Hotel (that being the ironic translation, considering what happened next) and asked if their chef could cook a fish I caught, a pair of young boys took an interest in the plastic bag I was holding. They were setting up a Christmas tree in the lobby with their mother.

Grabbing the dead moray behind the head, I pulled it out. The boys instantly screamed, and their mother ran for cover too.

"He says he can cook it," the desk clerk told me. She was on the phone.

I looked back at the terrified trio. They were cowering in the doorway to the adjacent lobby, their faces pale.

"It's *morto*," I tried to assure them, but they just stared at me like I was a lunatic. Then, when I tried to pass through that doorway to take the eel to the chef, they scattered like a bunch of juvies caught in the act of egging a house, each of them bolting in different directions.

If I needed any more proof of the panic monster fish can provoke, this was further evidence to add to my arsenal.

Following a plate of salivacious steamed mussels, the "buona murena fritta" arrived. That's what the chef called the eel, which had been sliced vertically in one-inch chunks and fried with the scales and skin intact. Beneath that perfect crust, the animated paisley pattern had finally been brought to a standstill. The spine bones were big and easy to spit out, and once I mastered the art of sucking the sweet, melt-in-your-mouth meat off the brittle skin, it was another unforgettable meal.

But the "sepia sashimi panini" (Luca's term) we had prepared out in the boat was even more memorable. Antonio had taken some rolls, cut them into buns, applied olive oil, then sliced some live squids we brought along for bait. He put the squid on the sandwiches, squeezed lemon on top of that, sprinkled salt and pepper, and finished them off with chopped parsley. The tentacles were still squiggling when I put them in my mouth, and they were damn tasty.

The real story, however, was in that juvenile tuna I photographed at the market, which I later found out wasn't a tuna. It was an Atlantic bonito, of which numerous studies agree that the average reproduction size is sixteen inches. The one I photographed was two inches short of that.

The IUCN lists this species in the category of "Least Concern," but they also state that "the majority of [this] fish landed in Turkey are below mature size, indicating that the stock will be unable to renew or sustain itself long-term."[2] Extending that logic, we arrive at the constant no-brainer: if you take too many immature fish out of a system, the species will crash.

The Reuters article "Ocean Fish Numbers on 'Brink of Collapse'— WWF" repeats the shocking figure of 75 percent, which is how much tuna, mackerel and bonito have crashed during a forty-two-year period ending in 2012.[3] Citing research from the Zoological Society of London, the website *Think Progress* not only concurs with the WWF, they incriminate the culprits as overfishing and climate change.[4]

But there I go again, retelling the same old narrative, which is what I've found to be the case from Borneo to Senegal to Italy, where I consistently recorded the overharvesting of immature fish. Seeing this firsthand led me to look harder at keystone species, which other species depend upon. At first I thought their exploitation was happening mainly in developing countries, but when you discover countries like Turkey and Italy taking the youngsters out, it's clear that industrialized countries are also taking part in the wiping out of fisheries.

And when you witness that destruction with your own eyes, it totally drives a message home. A message that only fools wouldn't heed. The translation of that message being: if we don't do something pronto, there goes the whole neighborhood.

In the meantime, the water is running red with blood. And it's not the blood of other people, and it's not the blood of other people's fish. It's the lifeblood from whence we came, and it's more than just a metaphor. It's where we're heading at breakneck speed, all in the name of short-term gain.

That's what I thought and that's what I got, now heading back to

Florence, New York, Arkansas, the entire pan-African-Amazonian-Caribbean-EU-U.S. experience of going after monster fish screaming in me to do something. Not as a desperate act of self-defense, but as a gesture that celebrates all that remains strange in the world. Because even if we have a history of doomed replication, and even if time has a way of being on time, we also have the inclination to preserve what mystifies and amazes us. So if we can find a way to put back more than we take out, then we definitely have a better chance at continuing to be part of this whole, holy, terrifying glory.

Terrifying because it's real, it's here, and vanishing.

And we are responsible.

Or not.

Conclusion

Fishery Solutions for the Disenlightenment

THE FIRST DOGFISH CAME IN AT DUSK, ITS TELLTALE DORSAL fin and sickle tail slashing through the frothing wave breaking on the sand. I'd caught it on salmon guts, a circle hook, eighty-pound braid, and a Carolina rig attached to my heavy-duty travel rod. It was three feet long and twisting and snapping all over the place as I held it by the tail. My twelve-year-old nephew was jumping up and down and I was equally as pumped.

We were off Point No Point, Washington, and the second one came in the next day at the same time. This one was four feet long. It was a twenty-something-pounder and my nephew and I had a blast examining it.

I didn't know it at the time, but the state record was only 20.25 pounds. So once again, I released a fish which could've been a record. That's what happens sometimes, but I'm okay with that since the real reward in meeting a fish is in letting it go.

Dogfish shark (or spiny dogfish or mud shark) range all over the world, and in the Pacific Northwest they're hardly regarded as respectable. The day before, a guy with a Hawaiian shirt and a neon-pink drink had wandered over. He told us they were catching them over at the lighthouse—"them" meaning salmon. But when I told him we were fishing for dogfish, he immediately turned and walked away without a

40. Spitzer and dogfish, Hansville, Washington.
Photo by Kraig Thayer Rasmussen.

word, obviously uncomfortable speaking to anyone who values such a lowly pest.

But dogfish have always been sacred to me. I've been catching them in Puget Sound all my life, always marveling that all it takes is a fish head or a bloody sculpin, and suddenly you've got three feet of furious, gnashing monster fish raging on the end of your line. Whereas the common reaction to dogfish isn't much different than Mr. Hawaiian Shirt's, I've always welcomed their sudden eruptions into my life. And because of my connection with this place, where generations of family created a history which I now know in my genomes like salmon returning home, dogfish always come with a rush of endorphins. Because of that, this fish is about as close as I can get to God.

I'm reminded of Chief Seattle, to whom the following quote is attributed: "Every part of this earth is sacred to my people. Every pine needle, every sandy shore, every mist in the dark woods, every clearing and humming insect is holy in the memory and experience of my people."[1] According to various sources, he also said, "Even the rocks, which seem to be dumb and dead as they swelter in the sun along the silent shore thrill with memories."[2]

Though I can't rightly claim the same degree of connection to this wilderness as the Suquamish people, I can claim a similar feeling for this area of the world and the fish that swim in it. That's how I feel about dogfish, and by extension, that's how I feel about all fish—because as Chief Seattle also supposedly said, echoing Buddha, "All things are connected."[3] That's why millions of us are concerned about the environment, and that's why the weirdest, wiggiest, most-loathed fish matter in the grand equation of interconnecting networks.

"What is man without the beasts?" Chief Seattle allegedly asked.[4]

To which I reply, "What are we without monster fish?"

Especially at this time in history when top predators are going down at a completely unsustainable rate. A rate that serves as a barometer for what all species are looking at as the shape of things to come.

Global warming isn't just increasing; it's accelerating. As *Business Insider* documented on May 21, 2016: "From 1958 to 2015 [the average global temperature] doubled to 0.015 degrees Celsius per year, and from February 1998 to February 2016 it rose by an average of 0.025 degrees Celsius per year! Time is truly running out."[5] And as Phys.org reports, seven of the world's top climate scientists have warned, "Earth is on track to sail past the two degree Celsius (3.6 degrees Fahrenheit) threshold for dangerous global warming by 2050."[6] And like idiots, we're letting this happen on our clock—which, according to *Bulletin of the Atomic Scientists*, "is now two minutes to midnight."[7] Aka, doomsday.

To make things even more complicated, the presiding officer of the U.S. government has appointed a new head of the EPA who the *New York Times* describes as "best pals with the oil and gas industry, and he knows the EPA mainly as an entity to be sued. Under his watchful eye, his state has allowed so much natural gas fracking that Oklahoma now has way more earthquakes than sunrises."[8] In that same issue of the *Times*, the Environmental Working Group stated that this climate-change denier will be "the most hostile EPA administrator toward clean air and safe drinking water in history."[9] Add to that a secretary of state who was ExxonMobil's chief executive and is raring to drill in the Arctic, a secretary of the interior who drove most of the National Park Service Advisory Board to resign in protest, and an entire administration hell-bent on deregulating the energy industry in favor of big oil and dirty coal, and the translation is that the environment, like civil rights, is about to be set a century back. And with global warming accelerating, the future's too close for that.

As I've mentioned before, our fisheries are the measure of our planet's health. And to measure the state of world fisheries, we need look no further than the "State of Fisheries Worldwide" report in *World Ocean Review*, published by the nonprofit Maribus company, who paint the following picture: "The results are alarming, because the pressure on fish populations has been escalating for years. According to the current SOFIA Report, the proportion of overexploited or depleted stocks has increased from 10 percent in 1974 to 29.9 percent in 2009. After temporary fluctuations, the proportion of fully exploited stocks rose during the same period of time, from 51 percent to 57 percent. . . . A clear trend is therefore emerging: as far as overfishing and the intensive exploitation of the oceans are concerned, the situation is not improving; it is slowly but steadily deteriorating."[10]

As for the measure of our freshwater fisheries, the journal *Fisheries* reports that biologists have reached consensus that "global climate change is altering freshwater ecosystems and affecting fish populations and communities." Documented findings in freshwater species include elevated "metabolic costs and decreasing growth and survival," "conditions outside of . . . optimal thermal range," "compromised immune function," "altered disease prevalence," and disruption of "hydromineral balance of fishes with narrow salinity tolerances," which affects "reproductive timing and . . . reproductive output and success." Furthermore, "These climate-induced environmental changes interact with . . . pollution, nonnative species, [and] habitat degradation . . . to directly or indirectly influence the physiological function of fishes." The result being, these combined factors "strongly influence evolutionary processes."[11]

That's the state of our fisheries: we are mutating the natural process of evolution by creating compromised species in deteriorating ecosystems on which the human race and all life on this planet depend for survival. Of course, all this is happening during an era of rapidly increasing technology and scientific discovery when we should be playing it smarter.

This brings me back to Chief Seattle, who I've been careful to quote, using words like "supposedly" and "allegedly" because we don't really know if he said those things. His famed speech of 1854 went through so many interpreters and translators that numerous contemporary scholars contest its authenticity.

In modern rhetoric, the term "fake news" is easily applied. Distortion of the facts has always been used for political purposes, but there's no disputing that this tactic is now at an all-time high. The last Bush administration made it a habit to distort, suppress, and omit climate-change data from the EPA's annual air pollution report, and the current administration makes it a practice to flat-out deceive the American public on a regular basis.[12] Examples of the latter include lies about creating "50,000 jobs in the coal sector" in 2017 and the air being "too clean for optimum health," and that's just for starters.[13] Such misinformation has had a major effect on public perception, and, in turn, on the future of everything Chief Seattle envisioned as worth preserving.

Thus, a century and a half after the apocrypha of Chief Seattle, the tendency of some one-percenters to deny and confound the facts that sustain all life on this planet is now subjecting every organism on this orb to the prospect of an unprecedented and accelerated annihilation. Meaning that in this era of mass extinction and extreme disinformation driven by the self-destructive urge to exploit our natural resources, if we're lucky enough to progress beyond the inevitable deluge our ecosystems are heading for, history will have no choice but to look back on this period and label it accordingly. And if that's the case, we'll be remembered as the fools who did the exact opposite of the spirit of the Enlightenment, which advocated tolerance, liberty, and the indisputable necessity of scientific discovery.

In other words, this is the Disenlightenment.

But seriously folks, we can lick this. We've got the ideas, we've got the brains, and if we can get to work in time, we've got the innovation and imagination necessary to save ourselves from ecocide. In my last fish book, I outlined the possibilities of iron fertilization, mariculture, creating greener gasoline from algae, methods to reflect sunlight back into space, planting mass forests to absorb carbon dioxide, and most importantly, ye olde fact that we can power the United States with just a thousand square miles of solar panels in the Desert Southwest.[14]

All these possibilities are still available, and they provide the opportunity to put a lot less stress on our resources while making a buck in the process. But there are hundreds of other options as well that can help us decrease the greenhouse gases eating away our atmosphere like tapeworms from the inside out.

Since there are all sorts of frightening figures for the damage done by jet fuel (like how there are nearly one hundred thousand flights per day, and how one jet taking off does as much damage as ten thousand cars idling in a traffic jam), let's take a look at this problem first. What can be verified is that particle emissions from aircraft are reduced when blended alternative fuels are used. According to NASA's ACCESS Program, "Jet-A" fuels lead to "a 50 percent reduction, or more, both on the ground and in the air."[15] One leading candidate for a more eco-friendly fuel is Isobutanal, which "can be produced out of corn starch, cellulosic materials, agricultural residues and other ethanol feedstocks."[16] Other renewable fuels can be made from pine trees, beets, and hemp. So wouldn't it be wise for those invested in flying the friendly skies to invest in developing these fields even further?

Hydrogen is another possibility. As an "emissions-free alternative fuel that can be produced from diverse domestic energy sources," the U.S. Department of Energy asserts that we have the potential to build a "hydrogen fueling infrastructure and produce hydrogen fuel cell electric vehicles" that are practical for widespread use.[17] Research is currently underway in both commercial and public sectors, and hydrogen-powered cars are on the streets and dawning on our consciousness.

And get this: not only have we sent a spacecraft beyond Mars using solar energy, and not only have we flown an aircraft around the world using solar power alone, but we now have a working prototype of a car that runs on water. It's in India right now with its inventor Moham-med Raees Markani behind the wheel. All he does is add a dash of calcium carbide to produce acetylene gas, and he's driving across town to meet with the "Chinese automobile companies to develop the idea further."[18] Since powering an 800 cc engine only costs fifteen cents per gallon, there's no reason why the automobile industries shouldn't profit from converting to this technology to preserve the ozone layer for as long as possible.

Meanwhile, there are tons of ideas to capitalize on for curbing climate change, which we need to get cracking on because the only hoax that can wipe out all life on this planet is the hoax that global warming is a hoax. The fact is we don't need toxic oil and coal; we've progressed beyond the need for such primitive energy sources. So basically, we have two choices: we can power this planet with solar and wind and calcium carbide and other alternative energy sources, or we can keep on killing ourselves by continuing to pledge allegiance to the flag of petrochemical suicide.

But for the conservation of fish specifically, let's start with a creative proactive idea spawned by a project known as Fishlove, which has suc-cessfully called attention to destruction from overfishing. In pairing seminude celebrities, both men and women, with totally naked fish, this nonprofit organization has created a series of portraits for the express purpose of "raising significant awareness for campaigns such as Marine Conservation Society, OCEAN 2012, Deep Sea Coalition, The End of the Line, and Blue Marine Foundation."[19] Each webpage provides sustain-ability information for the featured fish and the means to order prints. Fishlove reasons that "the collapse of fish stocks is an environmental catastrophe that is seen by scientists as being as important as climate change. But the good news is that it is a catastrophe that can be easily averted. With the right political measures over the next five years, our seas can survive for generations to come."

Here's the deal: whether your fetish be celebrities, conservation, nudity, or fish, Fishlove hooks its audience up with six commonsense consumer approaches for helping to sustain fisheries worldwide, which are deserving of being echoed. These include:

1. Diversify Your Choice: We're too reliant on the "Big Five": cod, haddock, tuna, salmon and prawns. Choose species such as coley or pouting instead of cod. Herring or sardines instead of tuna.

2. Shop at the Most Responsible Supermarkets: Buy your seafood from supermarkets awarded through our supermarket seafood survey; Sainsbury's and M S & S (gold), The Co-operative (silver) and Waitrose (bronze).

3. Look at Labels: The Marine Stewardship Council (M S C) seafood ecolabel recognises and rewards sustainable fishing and the Aquaculture Stewardship Council (A S C) certifies responsibly farmed seafood. The Marine Conservation Society recognises M S C and A S C certified as a better environmental choice for many seafood products.

4. Go Green: Choose fish caught using methods with lower environmental impact, such as hand lined or pot caught.

5. Choose Organic Farmed Seafood: Organic farms tend to have lower stocking densities, higher environmental standards and use feed sourced sustainably, so look for the organic label.

6. Avoid Eating Sharks and Deepwater Fish: Slow growing, long-lived species such as redfish and orange roughy breed slowly and are therefore vulnerable to over-exploitation. Fishing for deep sea fish can harm other sensitive species like coldwater coral that may never recover.[20]

In terms of the larger fish picture, however, the Ecosystem-Based Approach for Fishery Management (E B F M) was developed in reaction to the traditional single-species focused approach. Robert C. Francis et al. responded by developing the "Ten Commandments for Ecosystem-Based Fisheries Scientists," which was published in *Fisheries*:

1. Keep a perspective that is holistic, risk-averse, and adaptive.
2. Question key assumptions, no matter how basic.
3. Maintain old-growth age structure in fish populations.
4. Characterize and maintain the natural spatial structure of fish stocks.
5. Characterize and maintain viable fish habitats.
6. Characterize and maintain ecosystem resilience.
7. Identify and maintain critical food web connections.
8. Account for ecosystem change through time.
9. Account for evolutionary change caused by fishing.
10. Implement an approach that is integrated, interdisciplinary, and inclusive.[21]

These are certainly sound ideas to live by and definitely a starting point for policy makers. As Dr. Fikret Berkes argues in *Fish and Fisheries* regarding the implementation of EBFM, the concept is "revolutionary because it would involve dealing with multiple disciplines and multiple objectives . . . and expanding scope from management to governance . . . that includes cooperative, multilevel approaches involving partnerships, social learning and knowledge co-production."[22]

But the bullet points outlined by Francis et al. are the very source of the downfall of these fishery commandments. This quixotic document hinges on the expectation of cooperation in order to govern, and with all the divisive political and commercial conflicts of interest in the mix these days, finding common ground is virtually impossible. As a study in *Marine Policy* noted, "EBFM is 'holistic' and considers 'all factors,' but it is impossible for management to incorporate all factors into EBFM."[23] Reflectively, this is the same trouble we're still having with our original commandments.

Therefore, in the interest of developing a new list to bicker over, I offer the following no-nonsense solutions for saving our fish from the real monster we've created on this planet: the combination of global warming and the Disenlightenment.

1. No harvesting of juvenile fish anywhere, anytime, by anyone. Just outlaw it everywhere, starting with the 197 countries that signed on to the Paris Climate Accord.

2. If certain cultures insist on continuing to brew shark fin soup, then they should give the rest of those fish to those who need food, because shark is highly edible and shouldn't go to waste. Also, let's slap a hefty tax on each shark taken out of the system so as to develop shark farms to sustain wild populations.

3. And while we're at it, let's develop humane, safe aquaculture facilities for the fish we eat, because we know how to do it, and we've been doing it successfully for millennia. And since we presently farm tilapia, salmon, trout, catfish, zander, walleye, saugeye, paddlefish, sturgeon, gar, and myriad other fish en masse, why not profit from farming more?

4. Let's eat all those harmful invasive species disrupting our food chains. For example, bighead and silver carp have invaded the Mississippi River and have forced out 90 percent of the biomass in some Midwestern systems. Those fish are easily caught and they're excellent to eat—just ask the Chinese who've been farming them for five thousand years. All we need are processing plants which cost only a fraction of what's being spent on faulty electrical grids that can't even keep them out of the Great Lakes.

5. Let's pledge to put back more than we take out, both individually and as micro- and macro-communities, by actually putting more fish into contained systems than we ever thought possible. I'm talking "contained" so that hatchery-raised fish don't homogenize the genetics of wild populations. I'm also talking holding ponds, and converting lakes and marshlands into protected nesting and spawning habitats that can be used for both commercial and recreational fisheries.

Of course, naysayers will balk at these suggestions. They'll scream, "Ridiculous!" and, "How will we implement this?" and, "How will we enforce that?" They'll also note that we already know we need to protect our fisheries, so what new info does this give us?

But the thing is, the suggestions above, that's not where this study ends. I'm leaving those for others to consider while I issue a call to action, but not to my usual audience. I'm calling on those on the fence, who aren't completely convinced. I'm addressing those who wonder if they're doing enough, or if they're on the wrong side of history. That's right, I'm reaching out to you right now: those with ethical and moral questions about whether to accept responsibility or remain part of the problem. Because it's not that people *can* make a difference with oil spills and overfishing and all the planetary threats we face; it's that people *are* these industries, and change comes from the inside.

Another way of illustrating this unfortunate-but-true cliché is through the perspective that things might be tipping in favor of our fisheries, since it's not governments and economies making the major differences now. It's what's generally termed "the market."

I know, I know. Having spent my adolescence laying rubber in muscle cars and shaking my fist at "the Man," I can hardly believe I'm writing this. More so, I can hardly believe I believe this, but I do. The market has power, and because the market is made up of people, people can use that power to empower what Chief Seattle knew was not just sacred and beautiful, but vital to sustaining everything in our water.

For instance, it doesn't matter so much that our consistently bankrupt president (six times to be exact) is trying to revive the failing coal industry while doubling down on fossil fuels. As the *New York Times* reported in 2017, "Last year, the solar industry employed many more Americans than coal, while wind power topped 100,000 jobs."[24] And as *InsideClimate News* remarked that same year, "Twice as many Americans now work in the wind industry as in coal mining."[25] The results of this surge in renewable energies can be seen everywhere; there are wind farms across the country and solar panels from coast to coast attesting to the fact that we have the power to make traditional, ice-cap-melting forms of power—like petroleum and coal—obsolete.

But where we really witness evidence that alternative energy sources are the future is in the fact that the market can no longer deny science. Nope, because the market is made up of livelihoods and futures whose objective is to sustain the market and what the market sustains. Also, because sustaining the market depends on not automatically agreeing with the type of misinformation that indoctrinates the easily swayed, we are getting a lot better at not being snookered by lies. In this investment-based economy which depends on projecting operating costs and differentiating between long-term effects and trends, it just makes business sense to account for all factors involved and come up with creative solutions to persistent problems so they don't drive markets down. This can be seen in the ever-growing number of states, cities, universities, and businesses defying the United States pulling out from the Paris Climate Accord. That's why California's governor, Jerry Brown, teamed up with philanthropist Michael Bloomberg to—as the America's Pledge website states—"ensure the United States remains a global leader in reducing emissions and delivers the country's ambitious climate goals."[26] This is also why ExxonMobil and Conoco made a stand for staying in the Paris Climate Accord, just like plenty other corporations whose boards of directors can be voted out by stockholders (aka people) who refuse to tolerate climate-denying policies.

The term "socially responsible capitalism" is getting a lot of airplay these days because it's actually happening. Personally, I'm heartened by the number of new green businesses currently working to reform the market by reimagining the way we treat our natural resources. The financial firm Aspiration, for example, offers a highly competitive fossil-fuel-free bank account with interest rates a hundred times higher than the leading banks, plus free use of ATMs. They let clients decide their own fees, and they also provide a measurement tool "that lets you see your own personal Sustainability Score—the impact you're making on People and the Planet based on where you're shopping and spending every day."[27]

But that's only one example of the countless eco-conscious approaches now revolutionizing the way we do business on this planet. For example, Moon Willow Press, a small publisher in British Columbia, plants trees with profits from books, and I can't help thinking of the employee-owned New Belgium Beer in Fort Collins, Colorado, which, according to *Forbes*, "monitors and records all of its energy use, waste production and emissions and . . . reuses or composts more than 75% of the waste it produces in manufacturing" while making bicycles and a hybrid car available for employee use.[28]

The phone service CREDO Mobile is also impressive in this department. They state that "staying green is a core value" and they work "to reduce greenhouse gas emissions, including CO_2 emissions" while supporting "grassroots environmental action," "environmental non-profits," and recycling. They even took the activist initiative to install solar panels "directly in the proposed route of the Keystone XL pipeline to provide clean, renewable energy to farms and ranches that could be affected by pipeline construction."[29] But another thing they do is offer an alternative to corporations like Verizon and AT&T, who support anti-eco super PACs.[30]

My point is that there are millions of ecologically conscious individuals out there who want to see their money go to companies that pay it back to the environment. As the "Green Industry Analysis—Costs & Trends" report confirms, "55% of consumers across 60 countries are willing to pay higher prices for goods from environmentally conscious companies . . . [and] 71% of Americans . . . consider the environment as a factor when shopping."[31]

This might sound like a commercial, but since the businesses I've mentioned aren't paying me, it's not. But if it were a commercial, it would be for promoting a much greener commerce, which is what we need to sustain this rotating ball of water and earth. Granted, savvy people in the marketplace are making progressive changes right now, but we need more of that. Luckily for us, there's a demand for environmentally friendly enterprises to propel us where we need to go. Or, in the words of Al Gore, because of the visionary impetus for a more preservation-focused business climate, "market forces are working in our favor. Solar, wind, and other technologies are getting cheaper and better. More cities and companies are pledging to go 100 percent renewable . . . the sustainability revolution is unstoppable."[32]

My main question, however, is whether we have time enough to get things done when the ice is melting, the seas are rising, the sky is warming, and adding one degree more to the average oceanic temperature could very well make all our impassioned arguments moot.

So as the stingrays glide across the flats, and as the tarpons erupt in pure berserk leapery, and as the monster wels lurk through the murk of history, it just might be that our situation isn't as grim as it used to be due to an informed populace driving market forces. That's my optimistic take, and that's my hope, but it depends on whether the disenlightening forces at work will continue drilling and spilling and killing what we love with little restraint and respect for what this planet needs to survive.

It also depends on asking the questions that matter the most, then holding ourselves accountable when the solutions are as clear as our own reflections in the mirror. Reflections we see when we're brushing our teeth or fixing our hair. But mostly, reflections that measure what we value, which is the measurement by which we judge ourselves.

And that's how this narrative ends: by once again reversing the question because it can. You find yourself staring in the mirror. You find yourself wondering if the person looking back is giving back enough, or if you're just another tool burning up resources. And this question, it gets under your skin like a parasitical worm; it itches, it burns, it drives introspection—to the point that you can't trust your own responses.

This is something I know for certain. Because truthfully, despite my claim about doing this and writing this being good enough for me, it's not. What I realize now is that if we're seeking real solutions to real problems, we can't just invent easy answers to complex questions to mollify our fears. In other words, we must always search, we must always fight, we must always test the boundaries of ourselves in order to consider all angles for preserving the vanishing Wild. Because what I've discovered ultimately is that if we really give a damn about giving back, then no single answer will ever be enough to sustain the terrifying beauty of this mind-boggling, mind-blowing, mind-altering monster-fish world.

Notes

1. DEMYTHOLOGIZING DEMONOLOGIES

1. *Bizarre Foods*, season 2, episode 2, "Washington DC," directed by Andrew Zimmern, aired 2013 on Travel Channel.
2. *River Monsters*, season 6, episode 1, "Amazon Apocalypse," directed by Dominic Weston, aired April 6, 2014, on Animal Planet.
3. "Candiru Fish," Rainforest Expedition, accessed June 23, 2018, http://www.perunature.com/wp/candiru-fish-html.
4. *Frankenfish*, directed by Mark A. Z. Dippé (Columbia Tristar, 2004).
5. Michael Le Page, "Attack of the Killer Fish?" *New Scientist*, February 19, 2008, https://www.newscientist.com/blog/shortsharpscience/2008/02/attack-of-killer-fish.html.
6. John Odenkirk, "Northern Snakehead Fish, Invasive Species, May Not Be as Bad as Originally Thought," *Huffington Post*, May 30, 2013, https://www.huffingtonpost.com/2013/05/30/northern-snakehead-fish-invasive-species_n_3358192.html.
7. Le Page, "Attack of the Killer Fish?"
8. Theodore Roosevelt, *Through the Brazilian Wilderness* (Skyhorse Publishing, 2014), 41.
9. Roosevelt, *Through the Brazilian Wilderness*, 52, 53, 133.
10. Brian Clark Howard, "13 Scariest Freshwater Animals," *National Geographic*, accessed May 27, 2015, https://www.nationalgeographic.com/environment/photos/scariest-freshwater-animals.
11. "Piranha 'Less Deadly than Feared,'" BBC News, July 2, 2007, http://news.bbc.co.uk/2/hi/science/nature/6259946.stm.

12. *Piranha*, directed by Joe Dante (New World Pictures, 1978) and *Piranha 3DD*, directed by John Gulager (Dimension Films, 2012).

13. Eric J. Lyman, "Piranha Meat: It Can Take a Bite Out of What Ails You," *Houston Chronicle*, July 17, 1998, http://www.ericjlyman.com/piranha.html.

14. Roosevelt, *Through the Brazilian Wilderness*, 43.

2. WELSING FOR COLOSSALS

1. Cass Anderson, "Italian Bro Wearing NASCAR Gear Catches Catfish Big Enough to Swallow Ricky Bobby," *BroBible*, 2015, https://brobible.com /sports/article/wels-catfish-world-record-italy-po-delta.

2. Ellen Arnold, "A Big Fish Story," Ellen Arnold Photography, January 29, 2013, http://www.efarnold.com/adventureshoes/2013/01/29/a-big-fish-story.

3. "Loch Ness Monster Most Likely Large Catfish, Longtime Watcher Claims," *Fox News Science*, July 27, 2015, http://www.foxnews.com/science /2015/07/17/loch-ness-monster-most-likely-large-catfish-longtime -watcher-claims.html.

4. *National Audubon Society Field Guide to North American Fishes, Whales & Dolphins* (Alfred A. Knopf, 1995), 365.

5. Mark Spitzer, "Spitzer vs. Wels Catfish," August 10, 2015, video, 2:00, https://www.youtube.com/watch?v=-XuEXpCD9_w.

6. Hunter S. Thompson, quoted in Douglas Brinkley, "Football Season Is Over: Hunter S. Thompson, 1937–2005," *Rolling Stone Magazine*, September 22, 2005, https://www.rollingstone.com/culture/features/football -season-is-over-20050922.

7. Fishery Service, Directorate General of Forest Ecosystems and Environmental Management Ministry of Agriculture, Livestock, Fisheries and Food, email message to author via Google Translate, July 26, 2017.

8. Gobierno de Aragon, Departamento de Agricultura, Ganadería y Medio Ambiente, *Aragon General Fisheries Plan for 2012*, 2012, http://www.aragon.es/estaticos/GobiernoAragon/Departamentos /AgriculturaGanaderiaMedioAmbiente/MedioAmbiente/Areas/09_Pesca /fishGeneral_ENglish.pdf.

9. Nick Lloyd, "Invasive Fish Species in Spain," Iberia Nature, accessed February 8, 2018, http://www.iberianature.com/material/spaininvasivefish.htm.

3. CUDA CHAOS

1. "Report on Happiness and Satisfaction with Life," *Dominican Republic Live*, July 2009, http://www.dominican-republic-live.com/dominican -republic/news/year-2009/july-2009.html.

2. "Barracudas," Seaworld Parks & Entertainment, accessed March 14, 2016, https://seaworld.org/Animal-Info/Animal-Bytes/Bony-Fish/Barracudas.

3. Cathleen Bester, "Great Barracuda," Florida Museum of Natural History, University of Florida, accessed March 14, 2016, https://

www.floridamuseum.ufl.edu/fish/discover/species-profiles/sphyraena
-barracuda.

4. "Barracuda," Frost Museum of Science, accessed March 14, 2016, http://
www.frostscience.org/oceans/coralreef/predators/3barrcuda.html.

5. "Great Barracudas," MarineBio, accessed March 14, 2016, http://
marinebio.org/species.asp?id=108.

6. "Debunking the Myths Behind Barracuda," *Aqua Views Online Scuba
Magazine*, July 9, 2010, https://www.leisurepro.com/blog/scuba-guides
/debunking-myths-barracuda/.

7. Cathleen Bester, "Great Barracuda."

8. bpollackov, "40 LB BARACUDA JUMPS INTO FISHING BOAT!!!" May
6, 2012, video, 0:59, https://www.youtube.com/watch?v=bTw9QapciPg.

9. "*Sphyraena barracuda*," IUCN Red List of Threatened Species, accessed
March 14, 2016, http://dx.doi.org/10.2305/IUCN.UK.2015-4.RLTS
.T190399A15603115.en.

10. Mario Vargas Llosa, *Feast of the Goat* (Picador, 2000), 10.

4. SPORTFISHING GAR

1. *River Monsters*, season 5, episode 5, "Vampires of the Deep," directed by
Dominic Weston, aired 2014 on Animal Planet.

2. Mark Spitzer, *Season of the Gar* (University of Arkansas Press, 2010).

3. Mark Spitzer, *Return of the Gar* (University of North Texas Press, 2015).

4. Henry David Thoreau, "27 March (1848): Henry David Thoreau to
Harrison Blake," *American Reader*, accessed February 27, 2018, http://
theamericanreader.com/27-march-1848-henry-david-thoreau-to
-harrison-blake.

5. MONSTER-FISHING SHARK

1. E. Griffin, K. L. Miller, B. Freitas, and M. Hirshfield, *Predators as Prey:
Why Healthy Oceans Need Sharks* (Oceana, 2008), 3.

2. "A Quarter of Sharks and Rays Threatened with Extinction," International Union for Conservation of Nature, January 21, 2014, https://www
.iucn.org/content/quarter-sharks-and-rays-threatened-extinction; "More
Than Half of the Sharks, Rays and Chimaeras Native to the Mediter-
ranean Sea Are at Risk of Extinction," IUCN Red List of Threatened
Species, December 4, 2016, http://www.iucnredlist.org/news/more-than
-half-of-the-sharks-rays-and-chimaeras-native-to-the-mediterranean-sea
-are-at-risk-of-extinction.

3. Dennis Hevesi, "Frank Mundus, 82, Dies; Inspired 'Jaws,'" *New York
Times*, September 16, 2008, http://www.nytimes.com/2008/09/16
/nyregion/16mundus.html.

4. Tom Gregory, "Legendary Fisherman Frank Mundus' Last Interview,"
July 9, 2013, video, 4:29, https://youtu.be/32zRDO9yHpM.

5. "IDNR Stocks Alligator Gar as Part of Reintroduction Program," Illinois Department of Natural Resources, 2017, https://www.dnr.illinois.gov /news/Pages/idnr-Stocks-Alligator-Gar-as-Part-of-Reintroduction -Program.aspx.

6. Steve Smith, "Alabama Coosa River Spawning Striped Bass," Stripers247, 2011, https://www.stripers247.com/Alabama-Coosa-river-stripers.php.

7. Justin McCurry, "Warning Over Pacific Bluefin Tuna Stocks as Japan Meeting Ends in Stalemate," *Guardian*, September 4, 2015, https://www .theguardian.com/environment/2015/sep/04/warning-over-pacific-bluefin -tuna-stocks-as-japan-meeting-ends-in-stalemate.

8. "Global Marine Populations Slashed by Half," *Borneo Post*, September 17, 2015, http://www.theborneopost.com/2015/09/17/global-marine -populations-slashed-by-half.

9. "Failing Fisheries and Poor Ocean Health Starving Human Food Supply—Tide Must Turn," WWF Global, September 16, 2015, http:// wwf.panda.org/?252532/Failing-fisheries-and-poor-ocean-health-starving -human-food-supply—tide-must-turn.

10. Guy Harvey, "The Problem With Overfishing," *Alert Diver*, Winter 2010, http://www.alertdiver.com/260.

6. MONSTER CARP IN FRANCE

1. Izaak Walton, *The Compleat Angler* (Ecco, 1995), 153.

2. Kiersten Nunez, "Officials Say Removing Millions of Pounds of Carp from Utah Lake Will Net Big Financial Return," FOX 13 Salt Lake City, February 12, 2015, http://fox13now.com/2015/02/12/officials-say -removing-millions-of-pounds-of-carp-from-utah-lake-will-net-big -financial-return.

3. Jonathan Pearlman, "Australia Plans to Kill 'Plague' of European Carp with Herpes Virus," *Telegraph*, May 2, 2016, http://www.telegraph.co.uk /news/2016/05/02/australia-plans-to-kill-plague-of-european-carp-with -herpes-viru.

7. BANANAS FOR TARPON

1. "Tarpon Fishing," African Angler, http://www.african-angling.co.uk /Tarpon.htm.

2. Thomas McGuane, *The Longest Silence: A Life in Fishing* (Vintage, 2001), 13, ix.

3. Robert Hass, *Field Guide* (Yale University Press, 1998), 4.

4. Galway Kinnell, *Body Rags* (Houghton Mifflin, 1967), 63.

5. McGuane, *The Longest Silence*, xii.

6. Mark Longster, email message to author, October 18, 2016.

7. "*Megalops atlanticus*," IUCN Red List of Threatened Species, accessed October 1, 2016, http://dx.doi.org/10.2305/IUCN.UK.2012.RLTS .T191823A2006676.en.

8. Sean Morey, "*Megalops atlanticus*," Florida Museum of Natural History, University of Florida, accessed October 1, 2016, https://www
.floridamuseum.ufl.edu/fish/discover/species-profiles/megalops-atlanticus.

9. McGuane, *The Longest Silence*, x.

10. David Wallace-Wells, "The Uninhabitable Earth," *New York Magazine*, July 9, 2017, http://nymag.com/daily/intelligencer/2017/07/climate
-change-earth-too-hot-for-humans.html.

11. Chris Mooney, "The Arctic Is Full of Toxic Mercury and Climate Change Is Going to Release It," *Washington Post*, February 5, 2018, https://www
.washingtonpost.com/news/energy-environment/wp/2018/02/05/the
-arctic-is-full-of-toxic-mercury-and-climate-change-is-going-to-release-it
/?utm_term=.750cadfd9dd2.

8. STRIKING GOLD IN SENEGAL

1. "Billfish," Wikipedia, accessed October 22, 2016, https://en.wikipedia.org
/wiki/Billfish.

2. Zane Grey, *Tales of Fishes* (Starling and Black Publications, 2014), 87.

3. Grey, *Tales of Fishes*, 89.

4. Grey, *Tales of Fishes*, 97.

5. Grey, *Tales of Fishes*, 98.

6. Fiona Harvey, "Tuna and Mackerel Populations Suffer Catastrophic 74% Decline, Research Shows," *Guardian*, September 15, 2015, https://
www.theguardian.com/environment/2015/sep/15/tuna-and-mackerel
-populations-suffer-catastrophic-74-decline-research-shows.

7. "*Katsuwonus pelamis*," IUCN Red List of Threatened Species, accessed November 16, 2016, http://dx.doi.org/10.2305/IUCN.UK.2011-2.RLTS
.T170310A6739812.en.

8. Tracy McVeigh, "Overfished Tuna 'Near Extinction,'" *Guardian*, September 10, 2000, https://www.theguardian.com/environment/2000/sep/10
/food.fish.

9. "*Makaira nigricans*," IUCN Redlist of Threatened Species, accessed November 16, 2016, http://dx.doi.org/10.2305/IUCN.UK.2011-2.RLTS
.T170314A6743776.en.

10. *Explorer*, season 8, episode 5, "Call of the Wild," directed by Philip Boag, featuring David Gessner, aired January 10, 2016, on National Geographic.

11. Lewis Smith, "Supermarkets Warn That Yellowfin Tuna Will Collapse Without Urgent Action," *Fish2Fork*, April 13, 2016, http://fish2fork.com
/en_GB/news/news/supermarkets-warn-that-yellowfin-tuna-will-collapse
-without-urgent-action.

9. ATTACK OF THE ITALIAN ZANDER

1. "Monster Fish Killed after Terrorising Swimmers at Swiss Lake—and Served for Dinner," *Telegraph*, July 13, 2009, http://www.telegraph.co

.uk/news/newstopics/howaboutthat/5819633/Monster-fish-killed-after
-terrorising-swimmers-at-Swiss-lake-and-served-for-dinner.html.

2. "Zander," IGFA World Record Database, accessed November 2, 2016,
http://wrec.igfa.org/WRecordsList.aspx?lc=AllTackle&cn=Zander.

3. Mohamed bahig Fishing hunters, "Aggressive Zander Attacks Div-
ers," March 17, 2018, video, 4:30, https://www.youtube.com/watch?v=
TJiN9Wuwrmc. This webpage includes comments by Big Dog, Hoppy-
FishPerseo01, GPC, and Ed Dost.

4. Philippe Carrière, "Zander on the Nest Attack 3 Times," September 7,
2015, video, 0:40, https://www.youtube.com/watch?v=pjl2_-T0WJo.

5. Erich Varh, "Klopeiner See: Zander Attacks Diver," May 2, 2012, video,
1:10, https://www.youtube.com/watch?v=p9hkIJ_eVKs.

6. "Flight Carbon Footprint Calculator," Carbon Calculator, accessed February 12, 2018, https://calculator.carbonfootprint.com/calculator.aspx?tab=3.

7. "How Much Carbon Dioxide Is Produced From Burning Gasoline and
Diesel Fuel?" Independent Statistics & Analysis U.S. Energy Information
Administration, May 19, 2017, https://www.eia.gov/tools/faqs/faq.php?id
=307&t=11.

8. Robert Mauldin, email message to author, November 21, 2016.

9. "Global Warming Fast Facts," *National Geographic News*, June 14, 2007,
https://news.nationalgeographic.com/news/2004/12/1206_041206_global
_warming_2.html.

10. "Pledge of Resistance," Center for Biological Diversity, December 2, 2016, https://act.biologicaldiversity.org/onlineactions
/bdnz0fUpA0SQiKU3r1cFQg2.

10. TRANSLATING AN EELY IONIAN MONSTERFEST

1. Lydia Willgress, "That Giant Eel Wasn't Such a Monster After All! New
Photo Reveals '20ft' Fish Was Really Just 7ft All Along," *Daily Mail*,
May 15, 2016, http://www.dailymail.co.uk/news/article-3084377/New
-photo-reveals-20ft-conger-eel-just-trick-perspective-really-measured
-like-7ft.html.

2. "*Sarda sarda*," IUCN Red List of Threatened Species, accessed December
8, 2016, http://www.iucnredlist.org/details/155096/0.

3. Alister Doyle, "Ocean Fish Numbers on 'Brink of Collapse'—WWF,"
Reuters, September 16, 2015, https://www.reuters.com/article
/environment-oceans/ocean-fish-numbers-on-brink-of-collapse-wwf
-idUSL5N11M1UO20150916.

4. Jess Colarossi, "Climate Change and Overfishing Are Driving the World's
Oceans to the 'Brink of Collapse,'" *Think Progress*, September 18, 2015,
https://thinkprogress.org/climate-change-and-overfishing-are-driving-the
-worlds-oceans-to-the-brink-of-collapse-2d095e127640/#.8jcf0783q.

CONCLUSION

1. "Chief Seattle Speech: Did Chief Seattle Give the Environmental Speech He's Become Famous For?" Snopes, September 26, 2007, https://www .snopes.com/quotes/seattle.asp.
2. "Chief Seattle Speech: 'Chief Seattle's 1854 Oration'—ver. 1," Suquamish Tribe, accessed September 1, 2017, https://suquamish.nsn.us/home/about -us/chief-seattle-speech.
3. "Chief Seattle Speech," Snopes.
4. "Chief Seattle Speech," Snopes.
5. Henry Blodget, "It Has Not Been a Good Year for Global-Warming Skeptics," *Business Insider*, May 21, 2016, http://www.businessinsider.com /global-warming-is-accelerating-2016-5.
6. "Global Warming Set to Pass 2C Threshold in 2050: Report," Phys.org, Science X Network, September 29, 2016, https://phys.org/news/2016-09 -global-2c-threshold.html.
7. Rachel Bronson, "Statement from the President and CEO," 2018 Dooms- day Clock Statement, *Bulletin of the Atomic Scientists*, January 25, 2018, https://thebulletin.org/2018-doomsday-clock-statement.
8. Gail Collins, "Warming Up a New Staff and Climate," *New York Times*, December 9, 2016.
9. Coral Davenport and Eric Lipton, "Fossil Fuel Ally to Lead Environmen- tal Agency," *New York Times*, December 9, 2016.
10. "The Future of Fish: The Fisheries of the Future," *World Ocean Review*, 2013, http://worldoceanreview.com/en/wor-2/fisheries/state-of-fisheries -worldwide.
11. James E. Whitney et al., "Physiological Basis of Climate Change Impacts on North American Inland Fishes," *Fisheries* 41, no. 7 (July 2016): 334.
12. "Climate Change Research Distorted and Suppressed," Union of Con- cerned Scientists, June 2005, https://www.ucsusa.org/our-work/center -science-and-democracy/promoting-scientific-integrity/climate-change .html#.WoMBUOjwbIU; Chris Cillizza, "Donald Trump Says Some- thing That Isn't True 5.5 Times a Day. Every Day," *The Point with Chris Cillizza*, CNN Politics, November 14, 2017, https://www.cnn.com/2017 /11/14/politics/trump-fact-checker-1628/index.html.
13. Scott Pruitt, quoted in Louis Jacobson, "Are Coal Mining Jobs Up by 50,000 Since Last Year? Not Exactly," Politifact, June 5, 2017, http://www .politifact.com/truth-o-meter/statements/2017/jun/05/scott-pruitt/are -coal-mining-jobs-50000-last-year-not-exactly; Robert Phalen, quoted in Summer Meza, "Incoming EPA Adviser Thinks Air Is Too Clean," *News- week*, November 2, 2017, http://www.newsweek.com/robert-phalen-epa -air-too-clean-700143.

14. Mark Spitzer, *Beautifully Grotesque Fish of the American West* (University of Nebraska Press, 2017), 212–13.

15. Lillian Gipson, "NASA Reports Alternative Jet Fuel Research Results," National Aeronautics and Space Administration, January 9, 2015, https://www.nasa.gov/aero/nasa-reports-alternative-jet-fuel-research-results.html.

16. Michael Kanellos, "Can Isobutanol Replace Ethanol?" Green Tech Media, June 1, 2011, https://www.greentechmedia.com/articles/read/can-isobutanol-replace-ethanol#gs.ScF8M3A.

17. "Hydrogen," U.S. Department of Energy, accessed December 9, 2016, https://www.afdc.energy.gov/fuels/hydrogen.html.

18. Siobhan McFadyen, "Mechanic Invents 'Water Fuelled' Car That Runs for Less Than 2p a Litre," *Mirror*, January 3, 2016, https://www.mirror.co.uk/news/world-news/mechanic-invents-water-fuelled-car-7110769.

19. "Fishlove Releases New Series to Save Eel from Extinction and End Overfishing in EU," Fishlove, accessed December 9, 2016, https://fishlove.co.uk/.

20. "If You Love Fish," Fishlove, accessed December 9, 2016, https://fishlove.co.uk/what-you-can-do.html.

21. Robert C. Francis et al., "Ten Commandments for Ecosystem-Based Fisheries Scientists," *Fisheries* 32, no. 5 (May 2007): 217.

22. Fikret Berkes, "Implementing Ecosystem-Based Management: Evolution or Revolution?" *Fish and Fisheries* 13, no. 4 (December 2012): 465.

23. Ingrid S. Biedron and Barbara A. Knuth, "Toward Shared Understandings of Ecosystem-Based Fisheries Management Among Fishery Management Councils and Stakeholders in the U.S. Mid-Atlantic and New England Regions," *Marine Policy* 70 (2016): 40.

24. Nadja Popovich, "Today's Energy Jobs Are in Solar, Not Coal," *New York Times*, April 25, 2017.

25. Paul Horn, "U.S. Renewable Energy Jobs Employ 800,000+ People and Rising: In Charts," *InsideClimate News*, May 30, 2017, https://insideclimatenews.org/news/26052017/infographic-renewable-energy-jobs-worldwide-solar-wind-trump.

26. America's Pledge, accessed February 13, 2018, https://www.americaspledgeonclimate.com.

27. "Make the World a Better Place With Every Dollar You Spend," *Aspiration*, Aspiration Partners, Inc., accessed September 1, 2017, https://www.aspiration.com/summit/aim.

28. Susan Adams, "11 Companies Considered Best for the Environment," *Forbes*, April 22, 2014, https://www.forbes.com/sites/susanadams/2014/04/22/11-companies-considered-best-for-the-environment/#b72721a12ae9.

29. Trish Tobin, "At CREDO, Staying Green Is a Core Value," *CREDO Blog*, September 12, 2017, https://blog.credomobile.com/2017/09/at-credo-staying-green-is-a-core-value.

30. Kevin Matthews, "Which Corporations Just Pretend to Support Environmental Progress?" Care2, September 7, 2016, https://www.care2 .com/causes/which-corporations-just-pretend-to-support-environmental -progress.html.

31. "Green Industry Analysis 2018—Cost & Trends," Franchise Help, International Franchise Association, 2018, https://www.franchisehelp.com /industry-reports/green-industry-analysis-2018-cost-trends.

32. Al Gore, quoted in Brian Clark Howard, "Al Gore: The Green Revolution Is 'Unstoppable,'" *National Geographic*, July 7, 2017, https://www .nationalgeographic.com/magazine/2017/07/3-questions-al-gore-climate -change.